Bootstraps & Benefits

What the Right and Left

Understand about Poverty

and How We Can Work Together

for Lasting Solutions

SCOTT C. MILLER
Founder and CEO of Circles® USA

DENISE D. RHOADES
Hartsook Companies Inc.

Dedication

If you will start here and not stop until we move the needle on poverty, this book is dedicated to you.

Acknowledgements

We wish to thank the thousands of Circle Leaders on their journey out of poverty who are raising their prosperity IQ as they set goals and teach others what they know about poverty and the many more thousands of volunteers who are raising their poverty IQ as they serve Circle Leaders as friends and Circle Allies.

Table of Contents

Foreword

Jeannie Chaffin, president of Jeannie Chaffin, LLC, brings extensive experience in designing and executing strategies and policies that build communities and create opportunities for individuals and families with low incomes.

For five years, she led the Office of Community Services (OCS) as a senior executive service-level, presidential appointee in the U.S. Department of Health and Human Services. In her role as OCS director, she managed nearly $7 billion in federal block grants and discretionary funds and successfully led the Obama administration's efforts to strengthen the Community Services Block Grant (CSBG), the core funding for this nation's 1,000-plus Community Action Agencies.

Prior to her role as OCS director, Chaffin served as a senior policy advisor for the National Association for State Community Services Programs (NASCSP) where she worked with state CSBG directors and federal officials to implement services for individuals and families with low incomes.

Early in her career, Chaffin worked for the State of Missouri and at a local Community Action Agency in southwest Missouri where she administered CSBG and the Low-Income Home Energy Assistance Program (LIHEAP). She understands the challenges and opportunities that human service organizations face at the local, state, and national levels.

In her work across the country, Chaffin has engaged with diverse communities to set bold goals and solve complex socio-economic problems for communities and families with low incomes.

Jeannie Chaffin

I did not know it at the time, but many years ago, good fortune provided me with an incredible opportunity that shaped and influenced my perspective, career, and life. While still in college, I worked at a local Community Action Agency, where we helped connect individuals and families to services and endeavored to change the conditions in the community that were causing poverty. For me, there could not have been a better classroom. Every day, I had the opportunity to listen to people's life stories. And as I listened, I learned about their struggles.

Some worked multiple, low-wage jobs. For others—those without access to childcare or public transportation—working was beyond reach. Some had grown up in places where the school system failed them, and they could claim no marketable skills. Many had mental health challenges as a result of experiencing severe trauma as children. Yet, against this backdrop of adversity, people were fighting hard with what they had to gain some stability, protect their families, and help their children do a little better.

I also heard in their stories instances where individuals had made questionable life decisions. Research tells us that the stress and trauma of poverty can degrade a person's decision-making capabilities. But let's be honest: Who has not made a few missteps or had to learn a life lesson the hard way? I certainly did not always make the best decisions as a teenager and young adult, but my strong web of family and friends provided a buffer from the negative consequences of my inexperience and poor decisions.

The folks I met in those early days of my career helped me to see that the complexity of the causes and conditions of poverty demands that we find solutions that not only support individuals but also improve our communities, systems, and policies. I became a "Benefits" person, someone inclined to focus on what society can do to improve the circumstances of people with low incomes as opposed to a "Bootstraps" person who is inclined to focus on what individuals can do to improve their own circumstances. But I also learned that when it comes to eradicating poverty, as Scott and Denise write, it is a *both*, not an *either-or* proposition.

It has been my privilege to take that early good fortune and learning with me and put it to work, first at the state level, where I was responsible for the administration of several block grants designed to address poverty and later at a national association that supported state community service programs all across the country. Most recently, I had the honor of serving in the Obama administration, where I worked on policies and approaches that support individuals and families in their climb out of poverty and help communities across the country increase opportunities for their citizens.

Prevailing across all these roles, it has been my heart's desire that America would one day wake up and take action to eliminate the pain, suffering, wasted human potential, and unrealized economic growth brought on by poverty in this country—a nation where so much wealth exists. When you listen intently to individuals and families living in poverty and engage in relationships with them, you develop a different understanding of their circumstances and a deep desire to create change.

This book, *Bootstraps and Benefits*, with its suggestions for how we all can work together toward the eradication of poverty, comes to us at a critical moment in the great American experiment. We live in a rapidly changing and complex global world. The times demand that we tap into everyone's wisdom, gifts, knowledge, and skills, not just those who think and feel the same way we do. In this country of great wealth and abundance, we can do better. We must do better.

We hear much in the media today about political polarization, and it's no wonder: So many people stay in social media "bubbles," where they communicate only with people who think just like they do and seek their news and entertainment only from like-minded sources.

We urgently need new methods to burst these bubbles and encourage people to form real relationships where they listen and learn. I agree with *Bootstraps and Benefits* authors Scott Miller and Denise Rhoades that it is not necessary to convince people that one side is right, and the other is wrong; we simply need to start engaging *together*.

On January 10, 2017, President Obama gave a farewell address in Chicago. In his speech, he noted that our democracy needs every citizen and called for Americans to engage:

... It needs you. Not just when there's an election, not just when your own narrow interest is at stake, but over the full span of a lifetime. If you're tired of arguing with strangers on the internet, try talking with one of them in real life. If something needs fixing, then lace up your shoes, and do some organizing. If you're disappointed by your elected officials, grab a clipboard, get some signatures, and run for office yourself. Show up. Dive in. Stay at it.

Sometimes you'll win. Sometimes you'll lose. Presuming a reservoir of goodness in other people, that can be a risk, and there will be times when the process will disappoint you. But for those of us fortunate enough to have been a part of this work, and to see it up close, let me tell you, it can energize and inspire. And more often than not, your faith in America—and in Americans—will be confirmed.

Circles® USA (Circles) is a nationwide program for social change founded by Scott Miller. The Circles framework provides an opportunity for people to come together across class lines to learn about the conditions in their local communities that are holding families back. The Circles model puts families at the center and focuses on what it will take to support those with low incomes in their journey to reaching 200% of the Federal Poverty Guidelines (FPG).

Circles helps Bootstraps (inclined to focus on what individuals can do) and Benefits (inclined to focus on what society can do) wrestle together with the challenges families and communities face to find solutions that work.

Bootstraps and Benefits now provides a clear road map for how to move forward at the local level and engage others outside of our social spheres. *Bootstraps and Benefits* explains how communities can get started: Forming a Circles chapter and helping local families climb up the ladder can serve as a pathway to high-impact local and regional change.

In this book, Scott asks if America can push its prosperity rate up from 70% to something much higher. I say, yes, we can! And we must. It is essential to our American future to find ways to work across class, political, race, gender, and so many other divides to solve the complex and insidious challenges that face communities today.

Circles is currently engaged in scaling up from 59 chapters in 20 states and parts of Canada to 300 chapters in all 50 states to serve 10% of the United States' approximately 3000 counties. In each county, Circles is calling for a commitment to reduce poverty by at least 10% within 10 years. This is an audacious goal that has the potential to move the needle at the local level. Setting our compass on this North Star will lead us to new ways of thinking and bring people together around a common goal.

Finally, I want to underscore the importance of the foundational principles of both Circles and *Bootstraps and Benefits*: exchanging a culture of assumptions and allegations for one of personal relationships with one another. As Scott and Denise have illustrated so well, if we involve the *experts*—those individuals who are working hard, yet not getting ahead: "We might be surprised by their answers. We would surely learn more about the challenges of moving out of poverty than we ever knew."

Forming relationships, learning from one another, and working together to find new solutions—these are the pathways forward that will ensure we leave no one behind in our American story. This Benefits gal has her boots on and is ready to join with Bootstraps friends on the journey toward our shared destination.

Gary MacDougal is a businessman, writer, foundation director, former arts executive, and political leader. He has worked with governors, legislatures, and nonprofits for decades to assist the economically disadvantaged in moving from dependency to self-sufficiency.

Before attending Harvard Business School, MacDougal was a chief engineer of a Navy destroyer. He has also served as a trustee and as chairman of the Russell Sage Foundation in New York—a major funder of social science research with a primary focus on problems of poverty; trustee of the Annie E. Casey Foundation; and trustee of the W.T. Grant Foundation, which works with child development to address the problems of disadvantaged children.

MacDougal chaired the Illinois Governor's Task Force for Human Services Reform from 1993 to 1997. He was appointed by then-Vice President George H.W. Bush as senior advisor to his 1988 Presidential Campaign; appointed by President Bush as a public delegate of the United States to the United Nations for the 44th General Assembly session; appointed to the U.S. Commission on Improving the Effectiveness of the United Nations; and served on the U.S. Secretary of Labor's Commission on Workforce Quality and Labor Market Efficiency.

He is the author of *Make a Difference: A Spectacular Breakthrough in the Fight Against Poverty* and has published numerous articles on poverty and other topics in the *Wall Street Journal, New York Times, Washington Post, Chicago Tribune, Chicago Sun Times*, and *Harvard Business Review*, among others. He is a member of the Chicago Club, Harvard Club of New York City, the Council on Foreign Relations, the

Author's Guild, and is a former director of the Economic Club of Chicago.

Gary MacDougal

I am truly honored to be asked to include a foreword for *Bootstraps and Benefits*—a book that speaks to me because it is about a subject that has been at the top of my agenda for decades. This book's persuasive message is right on the mark.

I suppose, given my 17 years as CEO of a New York Stock Exchange-listed company with 5,000 employees, many would label me Bootstraps and, yes, I believe individual effort and hard work are the chief ingredients necessary for individuals to move out of poverty.

I also believe that a much-too-large proportion of government anti-poverty efforts does not use taxpayers' money effectively and, too often, may begin with good intentions but over time become driven by other interests. These other interests all too often include the well-being of individuals' own organizations, sometimes to the detriment of the needs of those seeking to move from dependency to self-sufficiency.

A river of money flows through government each year. Yet the many programs, started with the good intention of addressing poverty, are often fragmented, not integrated into local communities, not well connected to local employers, and the performance outcomes are rarely measured effectively. The result is wasted human potential and wasted taxpayer dollars.

Based on my many years of working in disadvantaged communities, especially in the minority neighborhoods in Chicago where I was born, I am convinced that the vast majority of those in poverty very much want to work and move themselves and their families toward a better life. Many face very tough barriers and would benefit immensely from Circles support in overcoming these challenges.

In his *Conservative Manifesto for the 1990s*, the conservative legend Paul Weyrich called poverty: "...the Achilles' heel of the free market." The richest country in the history of the world should not have large numbers of citizens in poverty. Many understand that a balanced Bootstraps and Benefits solution is needed, and that's why this book is necessary reading for responsible Americans.

At the heart of all this are real people whom most of us, including policymakers, rarely get to know. Conservatives need to recognize that large numbers of people in poverty and receiving government assistance really do want to work and have the same personal aspirations for themselves and their families as anyone else, but the bottom rungs aren't there on the ladder for moving up and out of poverty. Liberals need to recognize that much of the government funding spent to address poverty, however well intentioned, often goes toward managing poverty, not reducing it.

It may be hard for some people to appreciate just how tough the circumstances are for many disadvantaged people. Individuals who have grown up with stable resources may not understand the choices people living in survival mode might make. But by getting to know people in poverty, personally, I became a believer that if most of us started out with the disadvantages I saw, we would be stuck, too— unless we spotted some kind of ladder of opportunity and had a support system around us.

In my years of work as Chairman of the Illinois Governor's Task Force for Human Services Reform, I met with welfare recipients and came to understand that when nobody in a family or circle of friends and acquaintances is able to help you navigate the barriers in front of you, a Circles approach fills an absolutely crucial need. In Illinois, we established self-sufficiency coaches who were available 24/7 to help recipients find and retain work and navigate the challenges of childcare, transportation, and the many unforeseen circumstances that can prevent success. The lack of a competent, caring adult is all too common. Circles is one of the best models I've seen to fill this void.

Communities vary dramatically within a given city and across a state and nation. One size does *not* fit all. Only in communities can all the ingredients come together in a way to create a ladder of opportunity. In even the most impoverished communities, there are always wonderful people who will come together around the self-sufficiency challenge when it is presented.

One of the biggest surprises for me in working with anti-poverty efforts was facing an army of people who, at times, appeared more focused on managing poverty than eliminating it. Even many private-aid organizations receive much of their funding from government— local, state, and federal, and, unless they resist it, this creates a poverty industry, of sorts, that can become an end in itself. This is why great care must be taken to pay for specific, mission-minded, measured results, not organizational growth and activity.

Another missing rung on the ladder of opportunity is in the area of employment. Pockets of unemployment, even in the face of an overall strong demand for labor, have highlighted barriers for people in distressed communities that keep them from working. Some will criticize any focus on entry-level jobs. "Shouldn't we be worried about training people in the sophisticated skills needed by the American economy?" Of course we should, but what was your first job? Did it require sophisticated skills? Would it have supported a family of four? Did it lead directly to a well-paying job? Most first jobs are not sophisticated or well-paying. Mine was in a service station, pumping gas and cleaning restrooms.

For people in families where no one has worked for several generations, an entry-level job is a huge breakthrough—an important step not to be dismissed. It represents a first rung on the job ladder, albeit not where someone wants to stay forever. Overcoming the barriers necessary to get started, the soft skills developed, and the start of a resume all represent important, incremental steps forward.

On these and other related issues, *Bootstraps and Benefits* takes a frontline, granular view, and is an outstanding primer on precisely what is needed to help people move out of poverty. There are many insights offered, but the description of the Circles concepts and the Cliff Effect deserve special note.

The description of the Cliff Effect in this book is outstanding. Putting yourself in the shoes of a person struggling to escape poverty, one can imagine how distressing it must be to learn that the hard-earned pay raise you just achieved results in a worse household financial position due to the Cliff Effect. Help is badly needed in navigating this most unfortunate situation, and Circle Leaders' guidance is a big plus. Perhaps the graphic and persuasive arguments in this book can be used to generate badly needed change at both the state and national levels.

The bottom line is that this book should help persuade others, both Bootstraps and Benefits, to join the cause and help the many good people who share aspirations for themselves and their families to achieve a life free of poverty.

I have no doubt, there are enough well-meaning Americans out there willing to provide this Circles-type help. Coupled with state and federal human service systems, private-aid organizations, and the efforts of business, I believe we can meaningfully exceed this book's goal of reducing poverty by 10%.

Enjoy this interesting and important book!

Introduction

SCOTT MILLER, founder and CEO, Circles® USA

I gave a presentation at the Midwestern Governor's Association on Poverty. Denise Rhoades came up afterward and said, "Your message has remained consistent since I first heard it. That's a good thing." I'd met Denise many years earlier when she first learned about Circles. After hearing about Circles, she started teaching the Circle Leaders class and had done so for many years.

For someone like me, who has been accused over the years of creating too much change around me, it was refreshing to hear that my message had remained consistent. A series of phone conversations and visits with Denise and her husband, Marc, followed which led to the central theme of this book: Bootstraps and Benefits—how we all can work together for the common cause of eradicating poverty.

Simply defined:

- Bootstraps are persons inclined to focus on what individuals can do to improve their own circumstances.
- Benefits are persons inclined to focus on what society can do to improve the circumstances of groups of people.

When Denise told me her observation—that I am fluent in progressive/liberal, but can speak conservative with an accent—I was both amused and appreciative to have someone share such a unique perspective. I have a business degree and was raised by parents who always voted for whom they thought would make the best candidate, regardless of party affiliations.

My mother was an educator, and my dad was a businessman. This upbringing gave me an appreciation for different world views. I do believe that good systems produce good results and bring out the best in people. I also believe that personal initiative and growth is essential if one is to make the most of the opportunities before them.

I am equally frustrated with media on the right and left that have obvious political slants. I also find most mainstream political debates tedious, disappointing, and almost irrelevant to what the world really needs. When I listen to middle- and upper-income politicians, pundits, and policy wonks generate new ideas for addressing the chronic issues related to poverty, my mind simply explodes with the thought, "You are never going to get this right until you know people who have experienced poverty."

What we have done in our Circles work over the past 20 years is to give thousands of people the opportunity to build real, trusting, and respectful relationships across profoundly different socioeconomic class lines. People with abundant resources personally get to know people with insufficient resources and vice versa. They get together, they share world views, and arrive at insights and effective solutions to the problems of poverty.

One could say that the United States has accomplished a 70% success rate in generating prosperity for its citizens. However, more than 15% of U.S. households live below 100% of the FPG. If we double that rate to 30%, we come closer to estimating just how many households do not earn enough income to meet their basic needs and to set something aside for the future. The 70% rate is not bad, if we put our nation's history in proper context. We came from a European feudal system in which most people were poor. The United States was founded on the high ideals of democracy and meritocracy. These fundamental principles run deep in our psyches and remain intact due to our idealism that everything in life is possible, if we work for it.

I own this amazing optimism, so much so that I have built my career around the idea that our country can and should end poverty in our nation, in our lifetime. When one carries a contrary idea like this around and shares it with the world, it is fascinating to watch who shows up to provide critical pieces of the puzzle. My encounters with Denise and Marc have offered one of these significant pieces for solving poverty. We both share the belief that the left and right, together, have insights, values, and motivations to move the needle on ending poverty.

Can we push our prosperity rate up from 70% to something much higher? Of course we can. We have the most financially successful nation ever built in the history of humanity. Our gross domestic product towers over other nations. Our innovation is unparalleled in the world. We have a deep commitment to reward personal initiative as well as to provide a level playing field for everyone to succeed. Our commitment is for everyone to be able to pursue his or her happiness at the highest level possible and to realize his or her own American Dream. All these values and aspirations can contribute to the eventual eradication of poverty—if we can work together.

The strategies to ending poverty in the United States, while somewhat complex, are not the rocket science that the "experts" would have us believe. We have made it far too complicated to motivate people to take necessary actions. And we have allowed ourselves to be distracted by arguments that protect some of our cherished ideals and beliefs about Bootstraps and Benefits.

What the country needs is a straightforward agenda to end poverty. So, at the risk of sounding overly simplistic about how to fix a problem that the country has spent trillions of dollars not solving since the War on Poverty was launched fifty-plus years ago, let me break it down in this way:

- Understand that the biblical phrase, "…the poor will always be with you," does not mean, "don't address poverty." My theological colleagues have assured me that this quote is often taken out of context and should not be used as an excuse to do nothing.

- Address poverty as an economic development problem, not just as a humanitarian concern. The more qualified workers we have in our communities, the more we can attract and grow businesses. The greater number of good jobs there are, the less financial burden we carry as taxpayers. The economic development strategies in most communities are antiquated and must be updated to meet a rapidly changing economy. If our community does not have available jobs and qualified workers, poverty rates in that community will rise.

- Acknowledge that those of us who were raised in middle- and upper-income backgrounds typically have a poverty IQ that is too low to create effective policy without input from those who have lived it. We are not qualified to run anti-poverty programs on our own. We must have the input, guidance, and poverty IQ that those who have experienced poverty can bring to the table. Circles was codesigned by people who found ways out of poverty.

- Know that providing charity in isolation of long-term problem solving is typically counterproductive. The safety net must be tightly coupled with long-term goal setting, support, and career development. Do you ever wonder why food pantries and other organizations offering stop-gap assistance need more money every year? Are they referring people to programs that provide long-term supports and opportunities out of poverty? These are important questions to ask.

- Hold government and community programs financially accountable for producing long-term, out-of-poverty outcomes. If they assist people in earning 100% of the FPG, they receive compensation; 150% of the FPG, they receive additional compensation, and so on. Without a financial incentive to generate permanent solutions, many programs will continue to produce short-term outcomes that will not reduce poverty rates.

- Understand why government benefit programs should be administered by one agency, with one simplified in-take process of determining eligibility and with a simple prorated exit ramp as people earn more income. Currently, there are too many agencies running benefit programs with built-in disincentives that penalize people for earning too much income.

For example, if they make an extra dollar per hour, they lose all their childcare assistance and/or Medicaid, rather than a commensurate amount. Current benefit programs cause people to avoid new jobs and salary raises and, as currently designed, they guarantee a steady level of poverty in our nation. This is poor public policy and a waste of tax dollars. Even worse, it makes people squander valuable time navigating complex programs—time that could be spent on becoming self-sufficient.

- Appreciate that if people are going to move out of generational poverty, they are going to need jobs that they can handle, peer support from others who are succeeding, networking opportunities from volunteers with middle- and upper-income means, and a powerful game plan to overcome their personal barriers to obtaining, maintaining, and advancing in a good-paying job. A program such as Circles provides these supports. Without a complementary community-building strategy such as Circles, most programs do not have the staying power to interrupt generational poverty.

- Finally, if we want to increase our poverty IQ and make an effective contribution to the cause, we must find a way to form a relationship with someone who has experienced poverty. Without this, our ideas are likely to be off just enough to have the unintended consequence of delaying the real solutions to eradicating poverty.

Solving poverty requires a *both-and* rather than an *either-or* approach. This book is intended to provide structure for more meaningful dialogue that results in strategies to address poverty, to build community, and to allow more people to thrive.

Denise Rhoades, Hartsook Companies Inc.

After college, I returned to the Washington, D.C. area where I was born and raised. My first post-graduation job was on K Street two blocks from the White House. It was not unusual for the same persons experiencing homelessness to occupy the same locations along the same streets. As I grew more familiar with people along the way, this awareness became a constant preoccupation.

I did the things. The things you have done. The things we do: gave money, clothes, food. Whenever I had that gnawing sense I was bailing water on a sinking ship, I remembered the starfish: "It made a difference to that one."

Give me a break. I was 22, and I wanted to fix it.

Many decades later, I still want to fix it. Nothing's changed. Everything's changed.

You know the old saying: Not a liberal at twenty, no heart; still one at thirty, no head. It is an indelicate observation but a good jumping off place for how this book came to be: *Bootstraps and Benefits*.

Bootstraps: Persons inclined to focus on what individuals can do to improve their own circumstances.

Benefits: Persons inclined to focus on what society can do to improve the circumstances of groups of people.

I speak conservative fluently (Bootstraps), but I understand the language of the left (Benefits). Progressive/liberal is Scott Miller's first language, but he speaks conservative with an accent. We would disagree on a lot—if we had the time and inclination to do so—but we choose to invest our time and energy in addressing those things for which we have a shared endgame, defined language, and quantifiable goals tied to reducing poverty rates.

This is not about compromise or making concessions. It is not about negotiation. Bootstraps and Benefits is a transformational approach to addressing poverty that requires a seismic shift in focus from a tug of words and world views to leveraging our heads and hearts toward a shared endgame.

Taking a Bootstraps and Benefits approach does not mean watering down one's principles, so everyone is minimally satisfied and equally disappointed. It means going full-bore-collaboration mode on specific, measurable, well-defined, and shared goals where we bring the best of what we know and who we are and how we are wired to get a few things done.

Not all things. Not everything. A few (important) things.

Bootstraps (persons inclined to focus on what individuals can do to improve their own circumstances) and Benefits (persons inclined to focus on what society can do to improve the circumstances of groups of people) share common ground in the mission of Circles: Building community to end poverty one family at a time.

My husband, Marc, and I read Scott's book, *Until It's Gone*, around the same time we read Gary MacDougal's *Make a Difference*. Even though one author was Benefits and the other was Bootstraps, we noted a similar sense of urgency, genuineness, and shared insights around the issue of poverty.

As Gary has shared extensively over the years:

> "Most Americans agree that it's in all of our interest, for both humane and economic reasons, to help people move from dependency to self-sufficiency. The challenge is how to do it effectively while minimizing waste. Currently, our various anti-poverty efforts are both fragmented and overlapping." MacDougal, *New York Times*, October 2012

> "Many government programs should be combined, providing help to a family in need in a holistic way, … Outcomes must be measured wherever possible, the gold-standard question being: 'Did this effort change lives for the better and lead to self-sufficiency?' At present many programs are poorly measured or not measured at all." MacDougal, *Wall Street Journal*, September 2014

When we were first married, Marc worked in the Old Executive Office Building for the consummate Bootstraps president, Ronald Reagan, known to say: "We can't help everyone, but everyone can help someone." Decades later, when Marc heard about Circles, he shared it with me: "This makes sense," he said. High praise, since "makes sense" is Bootstraps for a cogent, no-nonsense plan with measurable goals and outcomes.

For Benefits, too, there is much to love about Circles, because it promotes an egalitarian structure where Circle Leaders—individuals working to move out of poverty—are always front and center. Allies—individuals volunteering to serve as intentional friends—come alongside Circle Leaders in their journey out of poverty.

They develop personal budgets. They identify systemic barriers. They talk about many subjects and learn from one another.

Everyone involved in the Circles community agrees and disagrees on all manner of things but, on this, they are of one mind: to see Circle Leaders succeed at achieving their goals for moving out of poverty permanently.

For well over 20 years, I have worked with Hartsook Companies Inc.—a professional fundraising firm with a global footprint serving nonprofits from every sector. My small piece of the puzzle has been to help nonprofits tell their stories and engage like-minded individuals to support the mission.

Demonstrating outcomes and raising money for the mission go hand in hand. Nonprofits should raise money based on their own local outcomes and ongoing success, not good intentions. If you are using the same success stories you used a year ago, it may be time to re-evaluate your program. What you actually do is your mission—not what you say you are going to do. What you achieve are your outcomes, not what you envision achieving. Donors want to invest in solutions, not needs. "The need is great!" is not a compelling case. Making a case means setting a specific goal and quantifying the dollar-to-goal need: "We have seen 20 families move out of poverty since we began. With support for an additional staff member we will be able to add another 20 families next year."

Here's what we know about donors: They don't want to invest in sandcastles. They want to invest their own money in demonstrated outcomes, not in anecdotal optimism and good intentions. They may be willing to direct OPM ("other people's money") toward new, unproven programs, but before writing checks out of their own accounts, funders ask great questions: "What are you going to do with this money? Are you using best practices? Who is doing this well already, and have those practices been put into place at your organization? How will you measure your progress, so we'll know you have achieved the goal?"

This is one of the many reasons why I became interested and served as a facilitator for the Circle Leaders' class for years: When done with fidelity, Circles chapters measure outcomes.

If you want to argue with people who do not agree with you, you can. There are plenty of people to argue with and places you can go to do so. But if you want to move the needle on poverty—whether you are Bootstraps or Benefits—welcome to the adventure of a lifetime.

Chapter 1

Going in Circles*

A glossary of terms is available at the end of the book.

Benefits—persons inclined to focus on what society can do to improve the circumstances of groups of people—will tell us that a lot more needs to be done to eliminate poverty.

Bootstraps—persons inclined to focus on what individuals can do to improve their own circumstances—will tell us that more than 50 years ago, the federal government launched an expensive, all-out War on Poverty and lost.

Benefits: "But at least we're trying!"

Bootstraps: "It failed."

Benefits: "Then we need to do more."

Bootstraps: "But not spend more."

Benefits: "Greedy!"

Bootstraps: "Naïve!"

Benefits: "They don't care."

Bootstraps: "They don't get it."

Bootstraps *or* Benefits

There are differing opinions and points of view among Bootstraps, just as there are among Benefits. Neither is a completely homogenous group.

Imagine drawing a circle around those with whom we agree on subject A.

After surveying this group on subject B, we exclude everyone with whom we disagree.

Now, ask about subject C, and so on.

Before long, we all would find ourselves in a circle of one.

Making broad generalizations for the purpose of demeaning others is uncivil. That is not Circles. But even making generalizations for the purpose of understanding one another can come with more risk than reward. Any attempt will be fraught with opportunities for misunderstanding and fault finding.

Yet, for those who would appreciate more of an explanation of what we mean by Bootstraps and Benefits, here are a few broad-stroke generalizations:

Benefits	Bootstraps
Expanded role and growth of government over a shrinking government	Limited role and growth of government over an expansion of government
"What can society do to improve the circumstances of groups of people?"	"What can individuals do to improve their own circumstances?"
Humanity is hard-wired for good. Trouble comes from without and must be overcome collectively.	Humanity is hard-wired for misbehavior. Trouble comes from within and must be overcome individually.
*"We want to help."	*"We want to be left alone."
*"Except when we don't."	

Bootstraps *and* Benefits

As Bootstraps and Benefits inflict each other with a perpetual tug of war of words, lobbing assumptions and allegations in both directions, families living with insufficient resources continue to struggle along—overwhelmed and heavy hearted.

Everywhere, there are people whose lives could be uplifted by having their Bootstraps and Benefits neighbors step away from their tugging and invest that time wisely. They could come alongside a struggling family and ask: "What's going on with you?"

Then listen, and be a friend.

These neighbors—let's call them John and Mary—don't care if their new friends hold to Keynesian or Austrian School economics. The only trickledown Mary is concerned about today is a water leak coming from the apartment above her. The aggregate demand John worries about this month is the cost of getting his car running and tank filled, so he can make it to work and not lose his job.

As Bootstraps and Benefits become personally connected with John's and Mary's struggles, they begin to share a new endgame: The leak fixed. The car running.

Those on the right and left will disagree about many things, but when they know John and Mary, and when they become personally involved in seeing them realize their financial and life goals, Bootstraps and Benefits no longer act as adversaries but as allies.

Maybe a War Isn't the Way

In the 1960s, declaring war on poverty was an expression of conviction and resolve. After decades of focusing on and talking about poverty and creating thousands of organizations dedicated to focusing on and talking about poverty, we are still managing poverty rather than reducing it.

What if we were to go to the experts?

No, not the heads of think tanks but the heads of homes where families are working hard but not getting ahead. What if we asked them, "What are your biggest struggles this week?" and then listened and lent a hand?

We might be surprised by their answers. We would surely learn more about the challenges of moving out of poverty than we ever knew.

Circle Leaders

Circles® USA is committed to building community to end poverty one family at a time.

Circle Leaders are individuals working to journey out of poverty with support from Circle Allies (volunteers who become intentional friends) and a supportive Circles community.

Allies provide relational support as Circle Leaders develop and implement plans for achieving their goals for financial self-sufficiency.

Rather than requesting a new program or another food box, what many Circle Leaders tell us is that what they need are friends who know things they do not. What we hear from Allies is that they learn more

35

and receive more out of their relationships with Circle Leaders than they give.

Circle Leaders and their families create and implement their goals for moving out of poverty permanently. At the same time, they help identify systemic barriers that make it hard for people to get ahead, including the unintended consequences of the Cliff Effect (Chapter 6, The Cliff Effect).

Circle Allies

Many of us want to be helpful, but we are reticent to overpromise and underproduce. Circles allows volunteers to take a step forward without fear of being overwhelmed by the commitment. Circles is a safe outlet for being helpful, because Allies are not on their own.

The structure provides clear boundaries, such as no exchange of money. Allies are not expected to know everything. They are friends, not mentors. Allies commit to an 18-month time frame and can continue after that or choose to move into a different volunteer role.

These personal, reciprocal relationships between Circle Leaders and their Allies may sound simple enough, but they are having a profound impact on individuals and families all over the country. People learn what they did not know about poverty and un-learn what they thought they knew.

Fact Finding, not Fault Finding

We do not have to agree on everything to do something, but we do need a framework of understanding—or we will spend the next 50 years spinning our wheels.

If we want to find someone to argue with, there's no shortage. There are plenty of opportunities to make assumptions and allegations. But not in Circles.

Taking a Bootstraps and Benefits approach means establishing a shared endgame where the objectives and parameters are clear, the language is defined, the outcomes are measured, and the process is adapted—over and over without an attitude of accusation or fault finding. Here is the process in brief:

- Establish a shared endgame.
- Define the terms.
- Set SMART goals (specific, measurable, achievable, relevant, and time-bound).
- Measure. Adapt. Measure. Adapt.

Not everyone will want to come along. Some prefer the tooth-wiggling nature of allegation and fault finding, but it is not productive.

Action Steps over Faction Cells

There are unlimited factions we can choose to endorse or condemn—pro-this, anti-that—but being drawn into a faction cell where we simply express our approval or disapproval is emotionally draining and unproductive. If we believe an issue is important, and that it is in our lane, i.e., coming at the right time and in our wheelhouse, then we should take action.

Action Steps

- Establish a shared endgame.
- Define the terms.
- Set SMART goals (specific, measurable, achievable, relevant, and time-bound).
- Measure. Adapt. Measure. Adapt.

Faction Cells

In a tooth-wiggling way, it may feel more satisfying simply to cheer or rage around a faction cell, but unless our interest is attached to action steps, it is a temporary emotional indulgence.

When we find ourselves investing valuable time, energy, and emotion in a faction cell, the quickest way out is to establish actions steps around a shared endgame, define the terms, set SMART goals, and then measure, adapt, measure, adapt …

Ask: "What it is it about this issue/faction that I care about? Is there something I could be doing or is this a distraction from what I should be doing? Is this in my lane?"

If there is something you need to do, then find people who care about the issue—and not necessarily those who see things exactly as you do. Other people may have information and insights you do not.

Having a clearly defined endgame puts us on track to accomplish something, or else it reveals that we did not want to do something as much as we wanted to *feel* something. That is good to know before we invest our time and energy simply cheering and raging.

Everyone's a moderate. No one's a moderate.

No one thinks their views are extreme. They are moderate, and everyone else is to their left or right.

It may sound counterintuitive, but some of the most intense conflicts in history have been between neighbors who are more similar to one another than they are to the rest of the world. What sounds like hair-splitting differences to someone halfway around the globe have prompted vicious rivalries.

In the United States, on a scale of anarchist (individualism to the extreme) to totalitarian (collectivism to the extreme), our Bootstraps and Benefits differences still leave us more alike than we may think. This is not to dismiss that there are opposing views or to diminish the importance of standing on principle and making a strong case for your position, but it does provide perspective.

Bootstraps and Benefits can invest the rest of their lives wrangling about poverty—that is certainly an option. Or they can invest that same time in being a friend and Circles Ally to a neighbor.

Not Compromise. Not Negotiation.

Taking a Bootstraps and Benefits approach is not about compromise. It is not about negotiation. It is an entirely different framework of understanding.

We all understand the language and culture of compromise: You give a little. I give a little. We add two variant lists, and divide by two.

We all understand the language and culture of negotiation: You pull one way. I pull the other way. We add two variant lists, and try to retain what we want and reject what we don't.

Neither is Circles.

Starting with a Shared Endgame

There is a time and place for compromise and negotiation but not in Circles.

The Circles endgame is to increase household earned income toward 200% of the FPG (Chapter 4, Targeting 200% of the FPG) and reduce poverty rates by 10% (Chapter 5, Targeting a 10% Reduction in Poverty).

We have neither the time nor the inclination for anything other than a shared endgame:

- Being personally supportive of Circle Leaders' goals as they increase their earned income toward 200% of the FPG
- Reducing poverty rates in our communities by 10%

It's what we do.

I was broke, broken, and homeless with three kids. Now, I have a home, money in the bank, attend school, and most of all, I have purpose. Circles was like a rescue team that came into my life while I was dying. They revived me, and I'm grateful.

LeAundrea Robinson, Circle Leader

Circles has exposed me to economic and social circumstances which I knew existed, but I didn't really understand all the personal implications of generational poverty until I got into Circles. Money alone will not break the cycle. It takes a community.

Bill Mitchell, Ally

Chapter 2

Endgame

The purpose of Circles has always been to build community to end poverty, but unless we inspect what we expect, it is impossible to know if we are moving the needle or just managing the problem.

Taking a Bootstraps and Benefits approach means starting with a shared endgame, not a hidden agenda—no matter how noble we believe our intentions and agendas to be.

To have a shared endgame, we establish specific goals, define the terms, measure the outcomes, and adapt the procedures based on the findings.

Circles' endgame is to reduce poverty rates by 10% as household incomes move toward 200% of the FPG.

All cards are on the table. No hidden agendas.

Everyday Heroes

Heroes do what others believe is impossible.

Addressing poverty may sound heroic, but even the phrase "ending poverty" can turn into a tug of words.

Benefits are inspired by the enormity of the goal: ending poverty.

Bootstraps prefer a more specific goal: ending poverty in Mary's life. Ending poverty in John's life. Ending poverty in the lives of as many individuals and families as possible.

Agree to disagree.

Whether we prefer to aim for the moon or beyond, we can focus on a specific, measurable, shared goal: a 10% reduction in poverty rates in our Circles community as households increase their earned income toward 200% of the FPG.

Action Steps, not Emotional Indulgence

Unfortunately, many of us try and convince others, who fundamentally disagree with us on eight things, to give up their opinions before we will work together on the two things on which we agree.

Too much time, energy, talent, and resources go into this tooth-wiggling effort. Neither one believes they will convince the other—nor will they be convinced.

So, why all the self-inflicted discomfort?

Because it is easier to battle over generalities beyond our control than it is to establish a specific target and be held accountable.

In addition, we are bombarded by 24/7 news and social media, which gives us a false sense of being informed—having just enough information to hold very strong opinions on everything but not enough personal knowledge to be wise.

Like an actor who has played a doctor on TV, we have lots to say on a lot of topics—but without scope, depth, or context. We sound informed but only to people who know as little as we do on a subject. TV doctors may be inspiring, but would we want one to perform surgery on us? Of course not.

Instead, if we focus our attention on what we do know and can do with a shared endgame before us, there is no time or energy left to argue inside the Circle—where John is sharing about his upcoming interview or Mary is talking about taking the GED test.

When we get it into our heads and hearts that this endgame is about Mary and John, not our own agendas, Bootstraps and Benefits can turn out to be bookends of brilliance.

Facts and Stats Are Pliable. Poverty Is Personal.

To be informed enough to take action effectively, we first must commit to a shared endgame and measure our outcomes. Only then will we know if we are reducing poverty or managing it.

- Circles supports households to achieve enough income to move out of poverty, typically at least 200% of the FPG. Bootstraps gravitate to this goal, because it emphasizes individual autonomy: "If we work hard, we can succeed. We have to pull ourselves up by the bootstraps."

- But, we also learn how systems can be transformed to support the eradication of poverty by pursuing a goal of reducing poverty rates by 10%. Benefits gravitate to this goal, because it emphasizes strategies that are large enough to make a difference in a systemic way, so people are less likely to remain stuck in poverty: "If the system's not working, it needs to be fixed to be fair."

We need a dual focus (not a "duel" focus) or we will continue to manage poverty rather than reduce it.

For the next 50 years, Bootstraps could focus on individuals' autonomy and not move the needle on poverty.

For the next 50 years, Benefits could focus on broken systems and not move the needle on poverty.

But what could happen if Bootstraps and Benefits were to focus on a shared endgame?

Agreed

In Circles all over the country, Bootstraps and Benefits are serving as friends and Circle Allies to Circle Leaders—individuals working hard to break out of poverty.

They share a meal together. They share their hopes and struggles. Both Allies and Circle Leaders support eachother as they take action steps toward their personal goals. At one of the weekly meetings, they hold a Big View meeting that is open to the public. Here, results are shared, and communitywide barriers are identified and solved.

This level of humility, vulnerability, and mutual support has a way of unleashing amazing insights. By addressing issues of poverty at a very personal level, Circles has uncovered surprising realities:

- Communities around the country have a "phantom workforce"—individuals who are willing and able to work but remain unemployed or underemployed due to circumstances many employers and institutions do not fully comprehend, i.e., lack of reliable transportation, lack of support systems for childcare when a child is sick, learning disabilities, fear of losing more in assistance than they are able to earn, and many other dire situations families in poverty know too well.

- The Cliff Effect - an immediate and dramatic drop-off in public assistance versus a sliding scale - creates disincentives that keep potential workers from moving forward for fear of placing their family in jeopardy. The Cliff Effect eliminates assistance faster than people can earn income to replace it.

- The challenges of a 1099-tax form economy where workers are contracted for jobs rather than employed by a company. They do not receive traditional benefits, such as vacation time or health insurance, and they pay their quarterly taxes rather than having them withheld from their paychecks. While this may be an exciting prospect for middle- and upper-income workers, it makes things more challenging for the working poor to move out of poverty. As companies replace employees with contracted workers, add automation, and take advantage of other cost-reducing strategies, individuals will need more support—the kind Circles provides—to access the information and skills necessary to transition into this new economic reality.

Finding Solutions

Today, communities are struggling with fewer economic-base jobs—those that bring money into the community and generate, on average, two local service jobs. These communities must recruit from a local, often unqualified, labor pool. Employers struggle to recruit the employees they need, because a phantom workforce will resist entry and middle-skill work opportunities until the Cliff Effect in assistance programs is mitigated or eliminated.

The Cliff Effect occurs when assistance programs such as childcare subsidies and Medicaid remove benefits faster than people can earn income to replace them. Not prorating the exit ramps off these programs creates a financial crisis for people as they earn more income.

Circles is building collaborations with organizations and policymakers across the country to understand the urgency of and benefits to eliminating the Cliff Effect.

To this end, we have developed the Cliff Effect Planning Tool^{TM} being beta-tested in nine states (Chapter 6, The Cliff Effect). This tool gives people the information they need to anticipate how increased income will affect their overall spending power as they leave benefit programs—before they fall off the financial cliff.

It also helps inform policymakers about the disincentives caused by programs that do not have prorated exit ramps, i.e., sliding scales for increased income and reduced benefits.

The Middle-skill Gap

Baby boomers continue to leave the workforce in massive numbers. Yet, more and more people are unqualified for a changing economy, creating a middle-skill gap in the workforce.

Circles understands the humanitarian nature (Benefits) of resolving poverty, as well as the economic imperative (Bootstraps).

Circle Leaders and Allies who sit side by side each week, gain insights on what it takes for people moving out of poverty to succeed in the workplace. Circles has learned how to recruit and train Allies to provide the much-needed support that Circle Leaders need, both inside and outside of work.

When the Boomers Bail

Economic-base jobs are those where the products and services provided are sold outside the state. These jobs bring new money into the economy and grow the economic pie. Every economic-base job is estimated to create one or two additional service-sector jobs.

Community Economics Lab (CELab) is a think tank based in Albuquerque, N.M. that innovates new approaches to economic development to work in a labor- and capital-constrained economy. CELab led a series of town halls throughout the state to help build a compelling economic assessment to recommend a pathway for state leaders in government, business, and philanthropy.

"It was the first time we have had consensus across the aisle and across the state about how many jobs we need to create, where those jobs should come from, and what specific improvements are required to make them happen," said Don Tripp, New Mexico Jobs Council co-chair and New Mexico's Speaker of the House of Representatives at the time.

A founding director of CELab, Mark Lautman, works with community leaders to transform community economies and to elevate the professional practice of economic and workforce development. He is the author of *When the Boomers Bail: A Community Economic Survival Guide.*

Lautman alerts communities to a serious economic threat. A structural shortage of qualified workers is creating a zero-sum labor market that forces communities to steal talent from each other to survive and grow.

Causes of this impending economic disaster include a baby boom generation that did not have enough children to replace themselves and an education system that has failed to properly prepare students for the demands of today's market.

Add to that the 78 million soon-to-be-retired baby boomers leaving the workforce and beginning to receive Social Security, and the situation worsens. Any areas unable to attract and retain talent will join a growing number of economically doomed communities.

It has become clear that the biggest barrier to economic development, at the community level, is the lack of qualified workers. Small communities will find it increasingly difficult to locate qualified workers, unless we discover ways to mine talent from the bottom third of a community's workforce population.

So far, the best and maybe the only program that works to employ the chronically poor and hard to employ—and has the critical elements to scale—is Circles.

Mark Lautman, co-founder, Community Economics Lab

Circles as a Workforce Solution

Circles® USA and the CELab have developed a new set of models to describe the intersection between economic development and anti-poverty work. Circles is now being cast as a workforce development solution that can solve the qualified labor challenges inherent in aggressive job creation plans, especially for depressed communities.

It is uncertain what the emerging economy will look like, but it is clear that the demand for qualified workers will mean a corresponding need for a network of support such as that provided by Circles for individuals moving into the workforce, out of poverty, and up the economic ladder.

All of the following are needed for individuals to move out poverty:

- Support from Allies (volunteers with middle- and/or upper-income means who can provide bridging capital) to achieve goals that produce an income at 200% or more of the FPG

- The education, training, and skills required for obtaining and retaining work, managing money, setting and achieving goals, and advancing in the workplace

- A safety-net system that has eliminated the Cliff Effect in benefit programs, so families can safely increase their earned income

- A community able to produce enough good-paying jobs for all of its residents who are willing and able to work

Community Currency

People in poverty are often experts at using existing community currency (bartering, co-ops, complementary commodities) in lieu of placing their families at risk due to the Cliff Effect. Anything that taps hidden and informal assets to realize unmet needs is identified and shared. What some might see as "getting around the system," others understand to be ingenious ways to navigate a flawed system.

Individuals with abundant resources understand this concept when it comes to using the tax code to follow the letter of the law (not always the intent) to avoid (not evade) paying taxes beyond what they know they must. What some might call shrewd, others might consider shady. This gray area of making the best of a bad situation is not unlike the daily challenge of those in poverty.

Someone who has grown up with stable resources—safe and sufficient food, shelter, clothes, and incidentals—might find it hard to understand why a person living in poverty would spend rather than save a $20 windfall. What they don't understand is what it is like to wonder, "What if I don't have another chance like this for a long time to make a purchase or go out to eat or to do something fun?" The random nature of "fun" makes spending the $20 a lot more logical when every day is about making it through today's difficulties to face tomorrow's hard knocks.

Friends and Allies

For Circle Leaders and their families, one of the most life-changing aspects of being part of a local Circles is the new and predictable nature of weekly meetings that are full of fun and supportive friends. Unlike programs where people are paid to be helpful, Circle Leaders and their families know their Allies are there because they enjoy them and care about them. It is uncanny how many Circle Leaders say that even after a long day at work, they do not want to miss going to Circles and, even if they did, their children would beg them to go.

At Circles, they share a meal. Childcare, with a robust children's program, is provided while Circle Leaders visit with Allies and others from the community. Here, they are asked for their insights and input. Here, they do important work and have fun doing it.

Circles provides an ideal environment for leveraging another kind of community currency—knowing a cross-section of people, making safe and supportive friendships that continue throughout the week, and having a cost-free place to go that their children enjoy.

I have had a powerhouse support team in my Allies. They were always there to support me in my decision making.

Lakeisha Wilson, Circle Leader

I enjoy spending time with my Circle Leader, and I'm thankful for our relationship. I am so proud of all she has accomplished, and I hope we will be lifelong friends!

Amy Murray, Ally

Chapter 3

Assumptions and Allegations

Bootstraps believe anything is possible. They look around and see what they perceive as opportunities. They ask: "What can individuals do now to improve their future?"

Benefits believe systems drive solutions. They look around and see what they perceive as challenges. They ask: "What can we all do now to improve our future?"

One of those descriptions may resonate with us more than the other. But whether Bootstraps or Benefits, we all can succumb to divisions, drama, assumptions, and allegations. Often, we are encouraged to do so via news and social media.

Our inclination for fight or flight leaves us with limited skills for dialogue—unless we have a shared endgame that is defined and measured.

If I want to go north and you want to go south, neither of us will be satisfied by going east or west (compromise).

If I want to go north and you want to go south, neither of us will be happy about being dragged in the opposite direction even a partial distance (negotiation).

But there are some roads Bootstraps and Benefits can travel together when the travel plans are not their own, but are John's and Mary's.

From a distance, stereotypes about one another are easy to make and even easier to maintain. But when Bootstraps and Benefits sit around the same table, share a meal, get on the same page about their Circle Leader's dreams and goals, and stay focused on those goals, rather than on ulterior agendas—the road map becomes self-evident.

What We're For Versus What We Fear

When people talk about what they are for, what is just as important, but less often shared and admitted to, is what they fear.

As it relates to poverty, Benefits fear that Bootstraps want to dismantle all safety nets and leave people vulnerable or worse. Bootstraps fear that Benefits want people to remain dependent on government safety nets to further an agenda.

Too often, Bootstraps and Benefits pull back hard on their own side of the rope to protect themselves and others from what they fear.

No one is naïve enough to think this tugging will end. It won't. Taking a Circles' Bootstraps and Benefits approach means being willing to drop the rope long enough to do something real and personal and meaningful, where there is a shared endgame.

It Is Easier to Be Mad Than Sad

As others have observed and expressed in different ways: It is easier to be mad than sad. Our brains—specifically the amygdala—release adrenaline when we are angry. Adrenaline increases our heart rate and blood flow. We, literally, feel more powerful when we are angry.

Allowing ourselves to identify and feel the "sad" masked by our "mad" requires vulnerability and humility, and it takes a higher level of self-control and intentionality.

For many of us, the sad behind our mad is rooted in what we fear. Learning how to recognize a personal sadness before it turns to anger, and then formulating a plan for addressing it, is an empowering process.

There is a time and place for fear and self-protection, but when utilized at the wrong time and place, it can be inhibiting, self-sabotaging, and unproductive.

Take It Outside

If you are Bootstraps, *be* Bootstraps—openly and authentically.

If you are Benefits, *be* Benefits—openly and authentically.

But when it comes to being a friend and Circles Ally to a Circle Leader who has bigger problems than debating Keynes and Hayek on economics, more urgent concerns than ageless controversies played out for a new generation, or hot-off-the-press "Butter Battles" on the conflict *de jour*, Bootstraps and Benefits can stop tugging and pull together.

There are many legitimate discussions to have but not here. Not in Circles. "Take it outside." Outside the Circle. In here, we are busy pulling in the same direction and learning from each other.

In Circles, I learned that I am not alone. I learned that I may be young, but I'm not dumb. I can do anything I put my mind to. Through Circles, I have become more aware of my resources and become a better friend and mother. As a Circle Leader, I've gotten not just one but two higher-paying jobs. Circles was the beginning of my accomplishments, but this is not the end!

55

Tori Franklin, Circle Leader

Circles has taught me the deep complexities of poverty. It has made me more aware of the critical issues that people in poverty must deal with every day.

Karen Bost, Ally

Inside the Circle

Inside the Circle, we have a shared endgame to see Mary realize her own goals and to see John turn lifelong dreams into reality.

Inside the Circle, we have too much to accomplish to let anyone distract us from the goal of seeing families move toward 200% of the Federal Poverty Guidelines, along with a 10% reduction in poverty rates in our Circles community. This is important stuff.

Inside the Circle, we:

- Use dialogue to learn more, not to show what we know.
- Leave buttons (titles) and banners (agendas) at the door.
- Assume that other Allies and volunteers are there to be helpful.
- Suspend assumptions and allegations.
- Ask questions to hear the responses—not to create a platform for our response.
- Listen.
- Handle conflicts privately to seek relational resolutions—not to attract an audience to our side.

Inside the Circle, we are:

- Focused on a shared endgame to increase household earned income toward 200% of the FPG and to reduce poverty rates by 10%
- Here to support Circle Leaders and their families—not to satisfy a need to be needed.
- Open to hearing new ideas and information.
- Dedicated to achieving long-term, economically stable results for families and communities.
- Committed to transparent and direct communication across socioeconomic lines to build transformative relationships.

Circles has helped me see the world and my life differently. I've learned how to save money and how to stop worrying so much about things that I can't change. As a Circle Leader, I have learned how to be a better mother to my four boys.

Megan Wilson, Circle Leader

There Will Be Challenging Moments

Even when there is a shared endgame, Bootstraps and Benefits will have challenging moments. What we choose to do when that happens is important. One option is to use Give 'em Five™—an interpersonal communication framework developed by Larry and Angela Thompson.

Larry is a speaker and author in the field of education and leadership training and the creator of Responsibility-Centered Discipline, Responsibility-Focused Leadership, and Responsibility-Centered Parenting. At a Circles National Conference, Larry shared his Give 'em Five conversation, which can be used in emotionally challenging moments.

Give 'em Five™

Every conflict or confrontation will look different. No two scenarios will be exactly alike, because no two people are alike. However, the process and principles of Give 'em Five remain consistent. The five components of a Give 'em Five conversation are:

- Support: Supportive comments given to and for the other person
- Expectation: Expectations shared by everyone in Circles based on the Circles culture followed with fidelity
- Breakdown: Breakdown of those expectations identified and shared with one another
- Benefit: Benefits to the other person. For example, "As we learn to communicate, even when we have differing opinions, it models these important lessons for our children and gives them skills they need to succeed."
- Closure: Closing the conversation, acknowledging any next steps

'We will be respectful, even when we don't agree.'

Since offering a "high-five" is a commonly understood gesture of support, it is a metaphor for the Give 'em Five conversation. It illustrates the motivation behind the conversation. It is a supportive message, especially in challenging moments: "I will be respectful of you, even when we don't agree." Here are important guidelines for using Give 'em Five:

- Use the other person's name during the conversation with the right tone and motivation—not to be condescending or manipulative.

- Take a listening position. The Give 'em Five conversation should be kept private rather than taking place in public to draw attention and support from those who agree with you. Make sure your posture and body language encourage, rather than detract from, the conversation. See yourself positioned physically and emotionally to be supportive.

- Monitor your voice volume. When we become agitated during a challenging moment, we tend to talk faster and louder. Often, our tone changes as well. Give 'em Five is intended to be a positive, supportive conversation, so tone matters.

- Protect the other person's "bubble." Because Give 'em Five needs to be a private conversation, it should take place out of earshot of others. It is equally important to stand a comfortable distance away. The other person will let you know if you are too close; they will lean back or step away. Be aware of this, and adjust.

These may sound like common-sense suggestions, but they are important. By keeping these principles in mind during challenging conversations, we also help keep our brains open and receptive to learning.

Implementing a Circles Culture

When we feel drawn into conflict, we can ask ourselves: "Am I fact finding or fault finding?" In a challenging moment, it may feel easier to find fault, but fanning conflict is more stressful in the long run, and it is not part of the Circles culture.

If we are fault finding, we should assess whether we want a Circles culture, with its shared endgame, or if what we really want is to use Circles to advance our own views and ulterior agenda.

- Am I on a fact-finding or fault-finding mission?

  If I am unsure …

- Do I want to know where you stand (fact finding), or do I want to put you in your place (fault finding)?

- Am I interested in hearing an alternate view (fact finding), or is my goal to shut down discussion (fault finding)?

- If I am wrong, do I really want to know?

  Whether fact finding or fault finding …

- What are the odds I could change your mind (on a particular subject) in the next two minutes?

- What are the odds you could change my mind (on a particular subject) in the next two minutes?

  If there is little chance to change the other person's mind in a brief amount of time …

- Do I want to discuss this privately outside of Circles?

Controversies will arise, but they do not have to turn into confrontation or conflict in Circles. We can disagree and move on: "I don't agree."

If it is worth a discussion, and both individuals want to discuss it, schedule a time to have a conversation outside of Circles. Or if it is a Circles-related issue appropriate for a public Big View meeting, bring in experts from alternative points of view.

Content, Intent, Text, and Context

A plumb line is a tool used to find a true vertical line on an upright surface. No matter how hard one might try to eyeball a straight line, our perceptions will be subjective. Gravity, along with a weighted plumb line, provides an objective point of view.

In a similar way, holding ourselves to a plumb line of consistency provides an objective vantage point for uncovering whether we are fault finding or fact finding.

Fault finding comes easily. Fact finding takes maturity, self-control, humility, consistency, and intellectual honesty. The most important question is: "If I'm wrong, do I want to know?" If the answer is yes, then I must be committed to applying a consistent plumb line. No one will do this perfectly all the time, but question is: "Do I want to be consistent?"

Here are four tests for assessing and, more importantly, disseminating information with consistency:

Content: Do I have a complete picture or just a piece of the puzzle?

Intent: Am I assigning intent based on facts or on what I am for or fear?

Text: Do I have the original information or an interpretation from someone who thinks and feels as I do?

Context: Do I have the original context or an interpretation from someone who thinks and feels as I do?

Fault Finding

- Insists on a public display versus private dialogue
- Makes statements without allowing for or encouraging discussion
- Uses interruptions, invectives, intimidation, mocking, or sarcasm to inhibit dialogue
- Employs theatrical body language (eyerolling, sighs, laughing, etc.) to express condescension
- Holds an ulterior, hidden endgame
- Dismisses another person's opinion as insignificant ("So, what?")
- Seeks to shut down and censure the views of others
- States opinions as facts ("Everyone knows …")
- Changes the meaning of words or parses them to misdirect
- Changes quotes, events, or context to frame things in a different way from the original intent of the quote, event, or context
- Makes allegations rather than shares specific information
- Assumes motives and creates a storyline about intent
- Assumes information not in evidence, i.e., hearsay, misquoted statements, etc.
- Makes a straw man argument (erroneous or distorted) and attacks a statement or position that has not been made
- Confuses correlation with causality: A and B may be correlated without one causing the other
- Dismisses 100% by pointing to an error of lesser significance: "She said 45.7 not 47.5, so focus on that and disregard everything else"

Fact Finding

- Initiates a private discussion
- Asks questions and listens
- Takes turns speaking and listening
- Presents a transparent endgame
- Seeks to understand the views of others
- Uses consistency as a plumb line: "If someone I was for did or said something similar, would I feel or react the same way?"
- Uses filters* for interpersonal communication

*Filters are based on Thompson's *Roadmap to Responsibility*. Everyone's filters will be a little different. The goal is to make it easier for the other person to receive our message while continuing to keep our minds and theirs open and receptive to learning.

Ask yourself:

- Would what I am about to say feel meaningful or helpful to me?
- Would I be OK with someone saying this (in this way) to someone I care about?
- If someone used this same manner with me, would I want to continue the conversation?

If the words you choose, the body language you project, or the tone and tenor you take would not motivate you, and you would not want it used with someone you care about, don't use it.

First Things First

Bootstraps and Benefits will have conflicts, but adults should be able to prioritize and put first things first.

For example, when facing challenges in our own lives, we know how to shift priorities from partisan to purposeful.

We would not choose a surgeon or mechanic based solely on our political inclinations.

No. We reprioritize.

The same thing holds true when our focus is on John or Mary. Our priorities change. We care. We think. We look around for solutions.

We put first things first, and we figure it out.

Hidden Rules

Over the years, Circles has been influenced by the work of Dr. Ruby Payne and Philip DeVol. Their insights on unspoken "hidden rules" among different socioeconomic groups (unwritten and unspoken cues and habits of the group), can be applied to Bootstraps and Benefits. All groups have their own hidden rules of what is expected and accepted and what is rejected by the group.

Hidden rules can create a sense of belonging. We know we are in a setting where we understand the hidden rules when we are not worried about being understood.

To the degree that we understand there are unspoken, hidden rules among Bootstraps and Benefits, we can have greater patience for ourselves and others as we learn about one another as individuals, not as stock characters or caricatures.

Both Bootstraps and Benefits are valued in Circles, because they bring the best of who they are and how they are wired to pull in the same direction for a shared endgame: households moving toward 200% of the FPG and a 10% reduction in poverty in a self-designated Circles area: city block, city, county, etc.

Allies and Circle Leaders are placed in Matched Circles—a Circle Leader and two or more Allies who meet to work on the Circle Leader's dreams, plans, and goals. It can take time for everyone to overcome long-held stereotypes. But as we learn about each other, oversimplified stereotypes are replaced with real-life understanding.

Whenever we feel pulled into a tug of war, we can choose to focus positively on principles—a shared endgame, measurable outcomes, etc.—rather than to focus negatively on people.

It is infinitely easier to romanticize or vilify groups of people than it is to build relationships and take action steps. The process cannot be forced, but it does happen over and over in Circles communities all over the country.

I started in Circles not knowing what to expect. I learned, regardless of my past, my future could be bright. As Circle Leaders, we set goals, and we are held accountable to fulfilling those goals.

I had a business plan that had been idle for five years. I knew I wanted to start a business, but I never thought I would be able to devote myself to something so big. But, to God be the glory, I can say I've found new confidence. I know my worth. I have awakened the fighter in me, and I am determined never to quit.

Through the support of Circles, my Allies, and my own self-determination, In Loving Hands Home Care Agency, LLC, was licensed and launched. I have numerous clients, and now I am putting many other people to work as well.

Although God's plans for me are far from over, I will continue to push forward and always remember to pay it forward. Today, my life is no longer about just surviving. I am finally thriving!

Ebony Clayborne, Circle Leader

Being a Circles Ally is like being a VIP on the floor at a Knicks game. You see the "thrill of victory" up-close-and-personal.

Ken Smith, Ally to Ebony

In Circles, I realized we were diverse in backgrounds, demographics, connections, and professions, but we all shared the same goal of being a friend, ally, and supporter of the Circles mission.

Circles is a safe place for having open dialogue, for learning about the far-reaching effects poverty has on families, and for becoming aware of the obstacles many face in navigating their way out of poverty.

I am thankful for being matched with Ebony and Ken. I'm so very proud of Ebony. She has encouraged me in so many ways. Thank you, Circles, for changing lives!

Angel Ellis, Ally to Ebony

Chapter 4

Targeting 200% of the FPG

The Federal Poverty Guidelines is not an ideal standard for assessing economic stability, but it serves as a metric for calculating a family's movement out of poverty. Circles uses the 200% target for the following reasons:

- It aims for twice as much earned income as the poverty guidelines suggest, and it is a good starting point for educating people about what is required for a family to have stable resources.

- It represents what most people really need to be self-sufficient, depending on the region of the country and whether people live in urban or rural communities.

- The math is simplified for Circle Leaders and Allies to begin conceptualizing the hourly rates and monthly income they need to formulate a plan and to realize their goals for self-sufficiency.

Since coming to Circles, we moved from an apartment that had water leaks, mold, and bugs to a nice house where we all have a bedroom.

Anonymous, youth participant whose family is in Circles

The Circles Children's Curriculum has been a lifesaver for our chapter. Having the topics and age-appropriate activities planned and ready to go takes the guesswork out and saves so much time.

We have been able to elevate our program with intentional, detailed plans for each age group and activities that take every type of learner into account. The children are developing confidence and lifelong skills. We're so grateful to have this addition to the Circles program.

Julie Duckett, Circles Coordinator
Circles, St. George, Utah

'What good are bootstraps, if you don't have boots?'

There is a big difference between helping people *in* poverty and helping people *out* of poverty. "Anti-poverty champions" (Benefits) should care as much about jobs as "business champions" (Bootstraps).

We cannot move the needle on poverty without talking about jobs. At the same time, moving out of poverty is not as simple as saying, "Get a job."

Denise:

My husband and I attended an event when we noticed a young woman sitting at a picnic table nearby. She was alone and crying. I walked over to check on her, and her story spilled out.

She and her boyfriend had moved from another state, because they heard a company in town was hiring. He had interviewed and gotten the job, but to secure the position, he'd had three days to return with steel-toed boots.

The couple had been depending on a relative for transportation and temporary housing, but the relational situation had gone south, and she was kicked out of the house.

The three days her boyfriend had been given to return with boots had come and gone. The company had filled the position. It is possible the employer also realized a lack of boots would not be this young man's last hurdle.

For those growing up with stable resources, this situation is hard to fathom: "Why would someone do this or that?" "Why not try this or that?" But for those growing up in crisis and instability, this story does not sound unusual or out of the ordinary at all. It's just life.

We helped her make stop-gap arrangements. She needed her birth certificate, so she could obtain a new Social Security card, so she could do the next thing. We got the first few steps checked off, but she and her boyfriend were making plans to move on.

They were used to making short-term decisions in survival mode. For them, moving on felt like the familiar thing to do. Taking a long-term approach would have required an enormous leap of faith—one they were not ready to make. This is another reason why Circles places an emphasis on individuals being "ready, able, and willing" (RAW) before becoming a Circle Leader. Perhaps "raw" from life's struggles, but all in for trying something new.

Circles Provides Stability and Support

People need jobs, and companies need workers. Sounds simple enough.

However, the organizations and agencies wanting to help and the individuals and families needing help often live in different worlds.

Rather than duplicating existing programs, Circles provides an organized community of support. This helps Circle Leaders access and integrate existing programs and services into their action steps for moving out of poverty.

In some communities, businesses reach out to their local Circles when they need employees. They know Circle Leaders are surrounded with the kind of adaptive, personalized support that government agencies and nonprofits do not have the capacity to provide.

Bonding and Bridging Capital

The relationships developed in Circles are not 9-to-5 formalities but are 24/7 friendships. Allies are not one-way mentors but are two-way friends where Circle Leaders give as much or more to the relationships as do their Allies.

Not only do Circle Leaders have bonding capital (connections a person has with friends and family), but through Circles, they grow in bridging capital (connections a person has with individuals other than friends and family).

Because we tend to know (or not know) the same kind of things as our friends and family, we are limited if we do not have enough bridging capital. With additional bridging capital, we can learn what we don't know, and our options are expanded.

Measuring Progress, Not Managing Poverty

Organizations and individuals who want to move the needle on poverty must balance their poverty IQ as well as their prosperity IQ.

Poverty IQ: Understanding poverty (living with insufficient resources) either through personal experience or through relationships with individuals who have experienced it firsthand.

Prosperity IQ: Understanding prosperity (acquiring, managing, and increasing resources) either through personal experience or through relationships with individuals who have experienced it firsthand.

Scott:

From the start, Circles has been about ending poverty. People join in on this adventure to end poverty with enthusiasm: "We're all for it!"

Yet when they hear, "Let's measure how we're doing," some become less enthusiastic: "No, thanks."

How can we be for families moving out of poverty permanently but push back against a target of earned income that is 200% of the FPG?

Eliminating poverty by 100% is exciting.

Reducing it by 10% (and measuring our progress) is hard work.

If we want to see communities thrive and families move out of poverty, we must stay focused on shared, measurable outcomes that encourage us to pull in the same direction.

'Somebody's got to do it'

As an engineer, my husband, Al, could see that Circles was a well-thought-out program and process. Our county needed something like this. Since he'd been a county commissioner, he knew we had several programs and food banks in the area, but we were treating symptoms. This was the first program we'd heard of that we thought could address underlying issues of poverty.

I said to Al, "Starting Circles in our community will require a lot of work." "Somebody's got to do it," he responded. And so, we did.

We were all a little nervous when we started. Some of our Circle Leaders were from fourth- and fifth-generation poverty. No one in their extended families knew what to do to move out of poverty. Some of them viewed middle-income Allies as rich. We knew it would take a lot of patience on everyone's part.

We have all learned a lot in the process. We have learned to listen. We have learned that it's not our job to tell each other what to do. It is a collaboration with shared goals. For many Circle Leaders, a goal is that their children would not grow up in generational poverty.

The first family we worked with is thriving, but it took several years for them to make it to this point. They had to give up relationships that were negative or even predatory. They were hard workers, but they were being taken advantage of by another family member who was not paying them for their work. These are the very real discussions that come up in Circles. This family still has hurdles to overcome, but overall, they are doing well.

According to our research, there are approximately 20,000 children in our county living under 200% of the poverty line. This is intolerable, and it is why we are focused on expanding (scaling up) Circles. If we can reduce poverty by 10% in our county over the next 10 years, it will change everything.

We work with adults, but our hope is to see their children make even greater strides. Now, Circle Leaders' children are saying things to them like, "Don't buy that expensive coffee. We can make coffee at home and save the money." Their children follow along with the age-appropriate Circles curriculum that someone in our Circles helped develop. They become part of the family discussion as they encourage their parents to set aside money, so they can go on the Circles day trips with Allies, for example.

Our local Community Action Agency partners with us. They support our budget with case managers, networking, and other resources. We utilize volunteers from churches and other community groups, but our partnerships with CAA and with Children and Youth Services make a big difference.

The chair of our Circles Recruitment Team works with Children and Youth Services. We asked her, "Of the children your agency is working to protect, what percentage are in poverty?" Her answer: "100%." It's why working together makes so much sense.

Other advantages in working with agencies already in place is that they are aware of grant opportunities—to keep the program sustainable—and they know individuals who are ready to become Circle Leaders. Unless someone is ready and willing to improve their financial status, we know they will not be able to move out of poverty.

We have heard from business owners and employers that there are not enough able-bodied workers for the jobs currently available. When he was a county commissioner, Al heard this all the time. Companies say, "The workforce is just not there." We say, "We can help you with this!" Our Allies are learning how to help their Circle Leaders find jobs and keep them. We help them with the unspoken rules they may encounter when working in a middle-income setting, but we do it all in a friendly and respectful way.

You can't do Circles successfully with only good-willed people. You need people in leadership roles who have relationships with others in every sector: business, education, workforce development, community services, etc. You need people who can bring others to the table.

We have the Workforce Development director from Penn College on our Circles Jobs and Education Team. We also have the school's chancellor and the directors of every educational department on that team as well. All of them are going through our Ally training.

Our Big View Team is educating our Circles community on the Cliff Effect Planning Tool. Then, we will bring in counselors to meet with Allies and families to create tailored paths out of poverty that include the best career plans for their specific situations.

We have relationships with businesses, and we're intentionally forming relationships with the top 25 employers in the area to share our Circle Leaders' success stories. We want employers to understand that we can provide them with dependable workers who have a strong support system around them. Moving forward, we want companies to look to Circles first to fill their job openings.

Reducing poverty by 10% in our county may not sound like a big number, but, wow! That will have an amazing impact. I'd be proud to have that etched on my gravestone! This is the kind of legacy we want to leave.

Al and Becky Ambrosini, Connellsville, Pa.

Chapter 5

Targeting a 10% Reduction in Poverty

Assuming you are not one already, imagine being asked to become a millionaire in 18 months.

"A millionaire?"

"Yes."

"That's impossible!"

"No, it's not impossible. People do it all the time."

What we mean when we say, "That's impossible" is: "That's impossible for me."

It's impossible for us, because we do not have the know-how necessary to get from here to there.

'Get a job!'

As impossible as the million-dollar request may sound, it is not so different from how people in poverty can feel when they are told to "get a job" that is adequate to live without government assistance. They do not see the stepping stones needed to get from where they are to where they want to be. "Get a job!" can feel as overwhelming and impossible as someone telling you to "Go become a millionaire!"

For people moving from poverty to financial stability, the chasm can be wider than many realize:

"Let's see, I'll need \$X an hour, and I'll have to get 40 hours a week (which is unlikely), which means I'll need my GED, which means I'll have to take classes, which means I'll need to pay for additional childcare, which means … Oh, well."

'But what if …?'

Now, back to the million-dollar goal.

Imagine, along with a target of becoming a millionaire in a year and a half, you are introduced to individuals who earned their first million in 18 months.

Not only are they willing to talk with you about their journey, but they have offered to meet with you on a regular basis.

And they really want to see you achieve your goal!

Is it still impossible?

Maybe, but it is likely you will be further along financially after 18 months by having had an ambitious target and motivated allies.

All In

The endgame of Circles is to develop a critical mass of Circles around the country that are committed to reducing poverty by 10% in their area by helping Circle Leaders move toward 200% of the FPG.

One of the reasons a 10% poverty reduction goal is used is because it is traditionally considered the minimal threshold for being "all in" on something.

Saying we want to reduce poverty by 100% is easier than actually reducing poverty by 10%. Using 10% also makes for simple math and focuses our actions and intentions on a specific, measurable goal.

Draw a Circle and Commit to Reducing Poverty by 10%

If a community wants to start a "Circles of This Geographic Area," they can locate current poverty rates for their self-designated region, move the decimal point one place, and know their target goal for reducing poverty by 10%.

If, however, they are more interested in managing poverty, they may want to start "Circles of a Bigger Geographical Area" but resist a goal of reducing poverty by 10% in that area. However—poverty management—would not be Circles done with fidelity.

Being all in on reducing poverty by 10% may cause us to consider encircling a smaller geographic area in order to hit the target. If we are all in, we will want to demonstrate results on a smaller scale before enlarging our Circle. Establishing a 10% goal demonstrates intent and influences our actions.

Set SMART Goals

Setting SMART goals is not for Circle Leaders and Allies only but for Circles chapters as well. Rather than taking on a task beyond their capacity to achieve, Circles chapters are encouraged to identify potential Circle Leaders who are ready, able, and willing to make big changes.

Individuals in a housing crisis, or just coming out of a drug abuse treatment program, may make successful Circle Leaders at a future time, but only when they are in a stable place and are well-prepared for the challenge.

Anything less makes the process more difficult for individuals instriving to move out of poverty. It also makes it harder for Allies and volunteers to be helpful, since their expectation is to support poverty elimination not poverty management.

The goal is to set Circle Leaders up for success, and inviting someone to start the process prematurely would not be helpful. As we have learned in Circles, feeling helpful and being helpful are different things.

Economic Imperative

Reducing poverty in the United States is no longer simply a humanitarian goal; it is an economic imperative. Yet, any solution—no matter how simple or beneficial—is hamstrung by partisan politics unless a collaborative approach is baked into the process from the beginning: Bootstraps and Benefits.

- Establish a shared endgame.
- Define the terms.
- Set SMART goals.
- Measure. Adapt. Measure. Adapt.

Otherwise, policies and programs swing back and forth from administration to administration, and people in poverty are left with perpetually new systems to learn and navigate: "No, we don't do it like that anymore."

Squeeze-the-balloon Pseudo-strategies

Many agencies and nonprofits work hard to help address issues of poverty, but for the most part, we have not been held accontable to demonstrate outcomes in poverty reduction.

Some programs and policies, intended to be helpful, offer "squeeze-the-balloon" pseudo-strategies, not real solutions. They may appear to fix one thing but only have squeezed the air from one place to another. The problem has not been solved, just moved.

By establishing a high bar of endgame targets, in tandem with a Bootstraps and Benefits approach to policies and ongoing data collection, Circles focuses on outcomes, not simply intentions. It emphasizes collaboration and innovation over partisan politics, and it stays fixed on a goal of movement toward success based on the 200% and 10% goals rather than on spending and activity. To achieve this elusive ideal, we should recognize the many obstacles that hold us back.

Staying Focused

In his book, *A Game Free Life* (karpmandramatriangle.com), psychotherapist, Dr. Stephen Karpman, explains the roles and interaction of the Drama Triangle:

Persecutor   Rescuer
"It's all your fault."   "You need me."

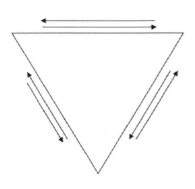

Victim
"Nothing's my fault."

Persecutor: Appears controlling, critical, angry, authoritative, rigid, and superior.

Rescuer: Needs to be needed. Enables others to remain dependent and gives them permission to fail; rescuing helps rescuers avoid facing their own issues.

Victim: Appears oppressed, helpless, powerless, ashamed—finding it difficult to make decisions or solve problems.

The Drama Triangle addresses perceptions of individuals as they shift back and forth between roles. The drama persists when it fulfills some unmet need for individuals to continue in conflict in lieu of addressing real issues, identifying solutions, and taking action.

Circles runs contrary to the Drama Triangle by discouraging Circle Leaders, Allies, and others from taking on persecutor, rescuer, or victim roles.

Allies are not mentors but friends. They are not tasked with telling Circle Leaders what to do (potential persecutor role) or with fixing Circle Leaders' problems (potential rescuer role). Circle Leaders are not victims. They are leaders of their own paths out of poverty.

In Circles, open conversations, a shared endgame, SMART goals, and mutual accountability mean working together to avoid drama and pulling together in the same direction.

The relational aspect of Circles is what sets it apart. There are so many classes and workshops out there, but in Circles, Circle Leaders and Allies are friends, not mentors and mentees. It's a different mindset. Allies aren't trying to fix Circle Leaders. Allies are there to be supportive.

Another difference is the time frame. Everyone in Circles has the time and space to learn and grow in genuine, incremental ways. We make sure that Circle Leaders and Allies understand they are committing themselves to an 18-month process, but you never have to leave Circles.

An important distinction is that Circles wraps its personalized support around an individual rather than individuals conforming to a program. Some programs seem to say, "What do you want from us?"

Others say, "What do we want from you?" In Circles, it is different. Each Circle Leader leads their own process. Things aren't handed to them. They do the work themselves with support from their Allies and the Circles community.

We want Circle Leaders to know what it means to be ready, able, and willing to make big life changes. Not everyone is ready. For example, if people have an undiagnosed mental health need, substance abuse issue, or they are in crisis, we direct them to the right place to receive help for their immediate needs. We want them to receive the appropriate help they need at the time.

We've found that many Circle Leaders who have struggled with depression start to realize how living in poverty and being in constant survival mode affects other areas. As they make friends and develop a plan for the future, many start feeling better physically and mentally, even before their financial situation starts to improve.

Circles of Greater Pittsburgh

Chapter 6

The Cliff Effect

The Cliff Effect represents one of the biggest barriers for individuals striving to move out of poverty. It creates a phantom workforce where individuals work fewer hours or below their potential, because benefits from assistance programs—food stamps/SNAP, childcare, cash assistance/TANF, utility assistance, housing/HUD and Medicaid—drop off at a faster rate than increases in earned income.

Without smooth offramps—sliding scales, prorated reductions, etc.—individuals who are working to increase their earned income run the risk of placing their families in greater financial jeopardy than if they earned less.

To significantly reduce poverty, families must earn an income at 200% or more of the FPG. Currently, for a family of three, this is approximately $40,000 or more annually.

Two Steps Forward ...

One effect of the Cliff Effect is perpetuating emotional and financial instability. People cannot plan and prepare as well for the future when they are in survival mode and in immediate danger of meeting basic needs.

Because the Cliff Effect is not widely understood, even among nonprofits and public-policy decision makers, most individuals and social service organizations never see it coming.

On the way to their goal of financial stability, families facing the Cliff Effect can become frustrated and discouraged—even when they know the financial cliff is right up the road.

The rush of pride in receiving a promotion from night shift to daytime hours or getting a bump in hourly pay is replaced with shock and anxiety when the childcare provider says, "You no longer qualify for assistance. You owe $X this month." That's when the math sets in: "So, I'm falling behind, financially, just to be away from my family even more?"

The major obstacle is that state and federal government assistance programs are not just complex, they are confusing and, at times, in conflict.

It is not a comprehensive, seamless system. It is a labyrinth filled with risks and unknowns.

Understanding the Cliff Effect

The Cliff Effect occurs when individuals increase their earned income but lose benefits at a rate that outpaces the increase. In addressing the Cliff Effect, tax rates also must be considered, because earned income is taxed, and benefits are not.

The Cliff Effect creates a phantom workforce where individuals who want to work and increase their earned income are hesitant to move forward for fear of placing their families in greater peril than if they "stayed put."

To navigate this economic challenge, Circles has created the one-of-a-kind Cliff Effect Planning Tool to help calculate and map a family's financial course out of poverty.

At the same time, Circles seeks to discuss the Cliff Effect with agencies and government officials at a macro-level to encourage interest and strategic thinking on the best solutions.

As Scott Miller shared before a New Mexico legislative committee: "Across the nation, policymakers and economics researchers from the right and left are looking for solutions that honor hard work, advance progress, and transition people off public benefits in a way that works."

Some options for addressing the Cliff Effect:

- Prorate benefit programs to eliminate disincentives for earning more income, i.e., creating a sliding scale for increased earnings to reduced benefits.

- Align and combine benefit programs with workforce development and, most importantly, with relationship-based support, so individuals and families have the personalized assistance and positive emotional involvement they need to navigate the cliff and move forward.

- Streamline the application and eligibility determinations so individuals can invest more time obtaining and retaining a job and less time navigating government requirements and meeting program deadlines.

'Do I want to see the Cliff Effect eliminated?'

No one would intentionally set families up to fail, but our current Rubik's Cube of state and federal government systems can have that net effect.

No one wants to discourage people from receiving a promotion at work and taking a pay increase, but many of the current systems do just that.

If you are tempted to point the finger at Bootstraps or Benefits, please pause, turn that finger around, and point to yourself as you answer these questions:

- "Do I want to see the Cliff Effect eliminated?" Let's assume you said yes.
- "Can lasting legislative solutions be implemented without buy-in from Bootstraps and Benefits?" Let's assume you said no.
- "Do I want a win (or loss) for Bootstraps, or do I want to see families win?"
- "Do I want a win (or loss) for Benefits, or do I want to see families win?"

87

If you chose families, Circles may be for you. In Circles, a WIN is not "What I need," but "What is needed."

Unleashing America's Phantom Workforce

A phantom workforce is comprised of individuals who could work, need to work, and want to work but who do not, because they fear losing benefits faster than they can increase their earned income. They know that once these benefits are lost, and their hours are cut, or they lose a job, they could be knocked back even more.

Going back through the labyrinth of filling out agency paperwork and finding time off work, reliable transportation, and last-minute childcare to pull it off is a nonstarter. It seems safer, wiser, and more responsible to one's family to keep the status quo (a lower income with benefits safely in place) than to take a chance of driving off the cliff: "Maybe we'll be the first people we know to make it over the chasm in one piece." Or maybe not.

Hard Facts, Soft Skills

Employers acknowledge that one of the biggest barriers to growth is finding and retaining qualified workers—those with soft skills around reliability and a willingness to learn.

Employers are willing to train new hires how to do a job, but they have neither the time nor the expertise to work around a shortage in soft skills.

This is where Circles provides a bridge over the chasm, between employers who need workers and individuals who need work. Employers are learning that Circle Leaders make good employees, because they have already proven to be ready, able, and willing to do what needs to be done, and they are encircled by a strong support system comprised of Allies and the local Circles community.

Planning Tools ... While We Resolve the Cliff Effect

Assistance programs use complex formulas. This makes it virtually impossible for a family with a low income or a community volunteer trying to assist them or even social services staff to determine, in advance, how much assistance individuals will lose if their income increases.

Losing benefits due to increased income, but at a disproportional rate of loss compared to increased income, has the unintentional consequence of blowing up the "survival budget" families depend on as they inch closer to a stable budget. Yet, in Circles, the goal is to achieve even more: a sufficient budget, where they have enough to meet their basic needs, save for emergencies, start saving for short-term goals, and invest for the future.

The Cliff Effect Planning Tool State by State

Circles volunteer Advisors David Priemer from Connellsville, Pa. and Vince Gonzales from Albuquerque, N.M. have created a prototype planning tool calibrated for all counties in nine states. The Cliff Effect Planning Tool helps predict losses in each of the major state and federal assistance programs for 18 levels of income.

Circle Leaders and volunteers fill out asset and demographic information. The Cliff Effect Planning Tool helps them know how financial adjustments will affect them in each of the public assistance programs. It examines and quantifies subsidies as Circle Leaders transition from their current income to their income goal of up to 200% of the FPG.

The Cliff Effect Planning Tool helps take the mystery out of the equation, so individuals can more effectively prepare for losses in benefits, while they continue to generate more earned income.

Cliff Effect Planning Tool

Circle Leader 1 Adults with 2 Children - Albuquerque, Bernalillo, New Mexico

CLIFF EFFECT ANALYSIS

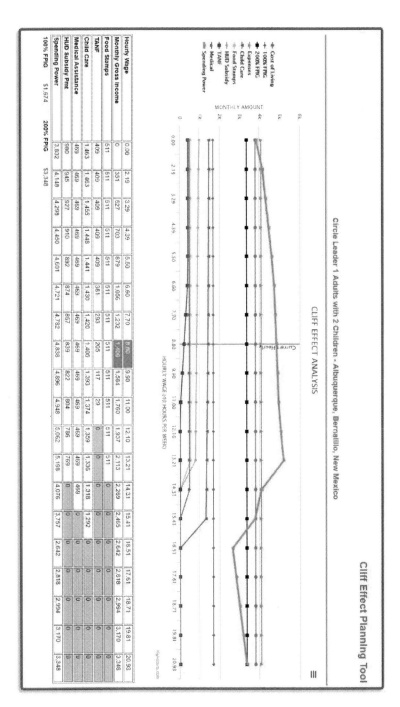

Legend: Cost of Living, 100% FPIG, 200% FPIG, Expenses, Child Care, Food Stamps, HUD Subsidy, TANF, Medical, Spending Power

MONTHLY AMOUNT — HOURLY WAGE (40 HOURS PER WEEK) — Current Amount

Hourly Wage	0.00	2.19	3.29	4.39	5.50	6.60	7.70	8.80	9.90	11.00	12.10	13.21	14.31	15.41	16.51	17.61	18.71	19.81	20.93
Monthly Gross Income	0	351	527	703	879	1,056	1,232	1,408	1,584	1,760	1,937	2,113	2,289	2,465	2,642	2,818	2,994	3,170	3,348
Food Stamps	511	511	511	511	511	511	511	511	511	511	511	511	0	0	0	0	0	0	0
TANF	409	409	409	409	409	381	293	205	117	29	0	0	0	0	0	0	0	0	0
Child Care	1,463	1,463	1,455	1,448	1,441	1,430	1,420	1,406	1,393	1,374	1,359	1,336	1,318	1,292	0	0	0	0	0
Medical Assistance	469	469	469	469	469	469	469	469	469	469	469	469	469	0	0	0	0	0	0
HUD Subsidy Pmt	980	945	927	910	892	874	857	839	822	804	785	769	0	0	0	0	0	0	0
Spending Power	3,832	4,148	4,298	4,450	4,601	4,721	4,782	4,838	4,896	4,948	5,062	5,198	4,076	3,757	2,642	2,818	2,994	3,170	3,348

	100% FPIG	200% FPIG
	$1,674	$3,348

Beyond the Tool: Resolving the Cliff Effect

Each year, billions of dollars are spent to manage the symptoms of poverty. Resolving the Cliff Effect is a great start at a solution that is good for everyone, especially employers and employees.

Employees do not do their best work when they are anxious about placing their family at financial risk. They do not make the best workers when they are worried that taking a promotion will cause them to lose their housing or when they are in immediate danger of meeting their basic needs.

While this proprietary Cliff Effect Planning Tool helps individuals navigate the Cliff Effect, a larger discussion is imperative. How do we resolve the Cliff Effect at the federal and state levels in a comprehensive, integrated way? How can the sheer dropoff be replaced with prorated schedules and smooth offramps including sliding scales and work-support assistance programs?

Eliminating the Cliff Effect: A Key to Economic Self-sufficiency

Circle Leaders throughout the United States, share stories about how their progress out of poverty remains impeded by policies that remove critical state and federal assistance programs before they have enough income to replace them.

These payment policies produce unnecessary crises and disincentives in the major government safety-net programs: food stamps/SNAP, childcare, cash assistance/TANF, utility assistance, housing/HUD and Medicaid.

The Cliff Effect Planning Tool is currently in beta-testing. Once completed, people leaving poverty and policymakers who run assistance programs will be able to see more clearly the problems caused by the Cliff Effect and make necessary changes.

Accountability = New Advocates

The Cliff Effect could be eliminated if assistance programs were held accountable to ensure household incomes move toward at least 200% of the FPG. The impetus to eliminate rather than manage poverty would create new advocates for addressing the Cliff Effect in a constructive and comprehensive way.

In the meantime, Circles is committed to promoting an alignment of incentives to achieve long-term results, so individuals are better able to transition off assistance programs, without the adverse impact of the Cliff Effect.

Feeling Helpful ≠ Being Helpful

Feeling helpful is self-satisfying. Therefore, the temptation is strong to say and do things that cause us to feel helpful. This is different from *being* helpful. To be helpful, what we say and do will be based on the Circle Leader's goals, not our own.

If we are serious about supporting Circle Leaders in achieving their financial goals, our actions will remain focused on a very specific target: Their plans and action steps for moving out of poverty permanently.

Making this switch in our heads and hearts requires intentionality. We let go of a short-term desire to feel helpful today and switch our focus to the Circle Leader's long-term goal of lasting financial stability and sustainability.

Imagine how helpful it will be for a family when they realize their objective of moving out of poverty permanently. That is the goal. That is being helpful.

One way that Circles is different from other programs is that we don't give things away. We don't hand out services. Circles is an empowering program. It's restoration versus temporary relief. Circle Leaders come because they want to improve their lives. We focus on relationships as part of a solution, not just as a side benefit.

Circles lets Circle Leaders think for themselves. They are their own agents of change. When you work toward something and achieve it, you feel empowered. You no longer feel dependent, and it feels good.

Circles takes people out of isolation, puts them into a community, and gives them many opportunities for leadership training. They become connected with people who are pulling in the same direction— developing healthy relationships and good boundaries.

They meet and grow close to people that they might never know otherwise. It gives them what we describe as bridging capital with people who have different information than they have.

Circle Leaders know that Allies, staff, and volunteers are there to be supportive, but not to give out money or do things for them that they can do for themselves.

Allies share their networks and put Circle Leaders in touch with a wider circle of people and information. We don't tell Circle Leaders what to do. We ask what they think is the right thing for them to do.

We brainstorm together on solutions rather than try to "solve their problems." Our goal is to be loving, not "liked." It is easier to enable than to be a supportive friend, but real love is doing the hard stuff together.

We screen Circle Leaders well on the front end. If they're not ready— if they are not an 8, 9, or 10 ready on a scale of 0 to 10— we don't have them start the process, because we don't want to set people up for disappointment. We invite them to come to our open meetings, like the Big View, for example, but to wait until their circumstances and outlook are at the right place for becoming a Circle Leader.

Some challenges Circle Leaders face come from their friends and families. Often, Circle Leaders face relational challenges as they begin to make changes: "You think you're better than us?" Learning to maintain good boundaries about money and expectations is something we talk about at Circles.

Other challenges include overcoming the effects of old ways of thinking that are learned when someone lives in survival mode. In survival mode, you think in terms of quick fixes. Circle Leaders set goals for the future. They start thinking ahead and begin making decisions based on their long-term goals. Like all of us, they are comfortable with what they know. It's hard to learn new things. That's why Circle Leader-Ally relationships—these friendships—are so valuable. It is a safe place to learn.

We see Circle Leaders facing many common challenges: lack of reliable transportation, so they can find and keep a job; lack of education to obtain the kind of job they need; limited work history; debt from payday loans; and the Cliff Effect.

That last one is big. When they're trying to work and move out of poverty, let's not send them off a cliff; let's make a hill.

We had a Circle Leader who had lost his union card through addiction. That was past him now, but his dream was to find work in his field. He was working in a different sector, but he'd advanced as far as he could in that job.

With encouragement from his Allies, he took a lower-paying job that was in his field with the goal of moving up. He went from managing others in one job to washing cars in another, because he had a long-term goal. It took awhile, but he got there, and he had folks cheering him on the whole time.

Circles of Joplin, Mo.

Chapter 7

About Circles

Circles® USA is an initiative with chapters in 20 states and parts of Canada, and it is still growing. Circles offers a unique relationship-based strategy that engages the entire community to move from poverty management to collaborative ownership of the solutions to poverty.

The Circles model works at both the individual and community level to:

- Empower motivated individuals to increase their prosperity IQ in order to move out of poverty and into stability.
- Increase the poverty IQ of leaders in business, education, health, philanthropy, volunteerism, public service, faith-based, and other sectors to motivate strategic action to resolve systemic barriers that households face in achieving economic stability.

Structure and Flexibility

Circles provides the organizational structure, expertise, and training for local Circles chapters. It leverages the power of community volunteers who establish intentional friendships with individuals ready, able, and willing to move out of poverty permanently.

At the same time, Circles addresses the barriers and challenges that make it difficult for individuals to move out of poverty. It provides the flexibility for chapters to be innovative and adaptive around the shared endgame, along with just enough structure to stay focused and effective.

Circle Leaders and Allies build two-way, reciprocal friendships. As Allies so often say, they receive as much or more from their friendships with Circle Leaders as they give.

Local Circles chapters hold weekly meetings where Circle Leaders, Allies, and members of the community come together to share a meal, host childcare and age-appropriate curricula, and build relationships across socioeconomic lines. They also discuss real-world obstacles and opportunities Circle Leaders face as they work to realize their financial goals for self-sufficiency.

As one Circle Leader offered, "We have changed our lives so profoundly that we will never move back into poverty again."

Unlike some programs, Circles isn't limited to one area of focus or fixed time restrictions. When Circle Leaders reach their goals, they can move into a new role as an Ally or volunteer and may reinvest what they've learned into the lives of others, but they never have to leave.

Local chapters have the flexibility to adapt and improve as they find ways to assist Circle Leaders in achieving their individualized goals for increased household earned income and the community goal of reducing poverty rates.

More and more, funders want to see results. There are a lot of groups that are relief based. They provide help to move people into stabilized housing and to supply food, clothes, and financial assistance.

People with insufficient resources already have to spend a lot of time and energy just maintaining—running here and there, filling out multiple forms, trying to satisfy the requirements of multiple agencies, often while trying to retain a low-income or part-time job and juggling transportation and childcare. We call it "agency time." It's time consuming, fragmented, confusing, frustrating, and exhausting.

Circles runs counter to agency time. Circles wraps around and adapts to the individual rather than the individual conforming to a program.

Most people would be surprised just how much time it takes for individuals to manage survival mode and that they have little to no time or energy left for moving out of poverty. Circles takes the approach that people aren't small parts of a complex, one-size-fits-all system—they are individuals with unique situations. Incremental growth is expected and celebrated.

Circles also provides a community space where there's a socio-economic mix—a place where everyone learns from one another.

Another difference in the Circles approach is that it is strength based rather than problem based. This makes a big difference, because it keeps the focus on Circle Leaders' personal goals for increased income, as well as other goals they determine for themselves.

Very often, people come to Circles feeling like the world is against them. Their life experiences have contributed to that perspective. They feel isolated—like no one could understand what they've been through.

At first, many have a difficult time communicating or even making eye contact. They see people around them who are open and optimistic, and it can feel foreign to them. It can be scary. They sit there and say, "I can't think of one 'New and Good' to share." And that's fine; everyone feels free to be real. But before too long, even if their circumstances haven't changed substantially, they begin to see things in a new way. Their attitude and outlook change, because now they have people around them who care about them personally.

At our Circles, we have "Circle Learners" who are taking the initial class. After that, they may become a Circle Leader, and after 18 months, they graduate to a Circle Alumni Group that provides volunteer support for Circles. They plan social events and meet together outside of Circles meetings. Each chapter has the freedom to do what works for them—as long as they adhere to the essentials and are committed to a shared endgame of increased household earned income and reduced poverty rates.

Here's what we would say to anyone considering Circles: "Approach it as a 'Learner'. Be prepared to learn a great deal about yourself and others. Set aside any rescuer mentality or mentor thinking. This is different. Circles is about reciprocity—everyone gives and receives. Sometimes Allies lose their jobs, and it's their Circle Leaders who show up with support and encouragement. Both Circle Leaders and Allies set SMART goals. Circles is an opportunity to unlearn unhealthy ideas about what it means to help."

One of the greatest things about Circles is its two-generational approach. Circle Leaders' children participate just as much as their parents. That their children love coming to Circles keeps parents motivated: "I wish I'd learned these things earlier in my life. I really want my children to have this."

At graduation, Circle Leaders share what they can do now that they couldn't do before: "I can get to work on time every day, because I have reliable transportation." "I can pay all my bills and have money left over to save." "I can set SMART goals and accomplish them." "Now, I can have fun with my kids, because I'm not always stressed out."

Circles of Holland, Mich.

Options

Growing up without stable resources can limit a child's opportunity to try new things or to practice, adjust, and improve their skills. This, along with frequent changes in living situations, schools, and caretakers can keep children from experiencing the natural, incremental learning curves that help them grow in confidence and competencies.

Even before Circle Leaders achieve their goals for financial stability, Circles helps counter some of a family's limitations by providing children with a variety of activities—and not just at Circles meetings. Circle Leaders, Allies, and their families often join in activities outside of Circles based on their shared interests.

From Stop-gap Assistance to Transformational Change

Circles represents a dramatic shift from static, stop-gap poverty management to transformational, relational change that takes place from the inside out. It fosters positive change for everyone—not just Circle Leaders. Change that is profound, organic, and lasting.

Circles is not a duplicate program or nonprofit. Circles offers a relationship-based clearinghouse for other programs and nonprofits. Rather than reproducing community services, Circles integrates Circle Leaders' personalized financial goals with existing resources—nonprofits, government agencies, schools, churches, businesses. Circles is a complement to, not in competition with, other agencies and organizations.

Not only do Circle Leaders find it easier to access existing resources—because they have Allies willing to help them navigate the process—but social service providers can benefit from the insights and expertise

Circle Leaders are willing to share: "That organization isn't open on the days and hours folks need them to be." "That agency never answers the phone." "That group is great, but they should think about..."

Lots of people in poverty don't want to be there, and they would do what it takes to get out, if they knew how ... that's what Circles provides.

Circle Leader, Grant County, Ind.

Circle Leaders at the Center

Circles provides a comprehensive program for people who are ready, able, and willing to move out of poverty. In the initial Circle Leaders' class, participants establish goals and make step-by-step plans for attaining those goals. They also acquire new tools and skills for securing and sustaining better jobs.

Once they complete the Circle Leaders' class, each Circle Leader is matched with two community volunteers—their Allies. Then, they attend weekly meetings where they work on their goals for moving toward 200% of the FPG.

Building Social Capital

A key to the success of Circles is matching Allies with Circle Leaders for at least 18 months as they implement their personalized plans. Allies offer coaching, job leads, problem solving help, and the encouragement required to secure and retain good jobs.

Circle Leaders expand their bridging capital—the connections a person has with individuals other than friends and family—as their Allies provide access to new social networks, which are often wider, stronger, and more diverse.

Becoming a Circles Community

While the Circle Leader remains at the center, it is the collective effort of families and the community surrounding them that is essential to ending poverty.

- Individuals are unique. One-size-fits-all programs fall short.
- Individuals are relational. Transactional programs— supplying services and information only—fall short.
- When systems incentivize an action or an inaction, individuals will choose that action or inaction. Work and savings should not be de-incentivized.
- When social service agencies and philanthropic funding is tied to reductions in poverty versus spending and activity, it will change how agencies spend their time and money.

Circles brings communities through distinct stages of development:

- Assessment: Asking questions. "Is Circles right for your community? Do you have the leadership and resources to start a Circles program in your area?" "Are you committed to a shared endgame of seeing households move to 200% of the FPG, along with a 10% reduction in poverty rates in your Circles area?"

- Planning: Getting started. If your community is ready and willing to start Circles, you will enter into a planning agreement with Circles® USA to lay the foundation.

- Demonstration: Taking action. You are now implementing one group of Circles to support families out of poverty, collecting data, and assessing outcomes. You are asking: "How is it working in our community? Are we seeing results? Have we been able to secure resources to sustain and grow the Circles program?"

- Expansion: Moving forward. You are happy with the results and can see the potential of growing Circles in your community.

Theory of Change

Lasting change does not come easily, even when we have stable resources and a strong support system. Yet, some circumstances make lasting change even more difficult.

Trauma, either directly or indirectly associated with growing up in poverty, can create heightened levels of self-protection. Trauma can cause us to become so self-protective that we limit our actions and expectations in a way that keeps us from setting or attaining goals.

Much of what works for survival and self-protection—either fight or flight—runs contrary to setting SMART goals.

Taking a "back door"—returning to what we know and what feels comfortable, rather than continuing to pursue our SMART goals—is always tempting. Back doors are continually calling out to us: "Run!"

'Stay!'

This is why a taking a relational, transformational approach is more effective than providing transactional programs, i.e., stop-gap supplies and information only. People need plenty of time and safe relationships where they can *process* the process of integrating new information into their lives.

Three helpful hints for Circle Leaders facing the urge to run out a "back door": Stay put—put everything on the table—table big decisions.

- *Stay put.* Change is hard. Even when we try to run from our problems, we take ourselves and our problems with us. Especially when we are scared or stressed (SOS), the temptation for fight or flight is strong. A good rule of thumb is to consider the counterintuitive choice: If, emotionally, we want to fight, we should consider walking away, thinking it through, and making an intentional decision. If, emotionally, we want to flee, we should consider staying put, thinking it through, and making an intentional decision. Either way, we should discuss the situation with Allies at the next Matched Circles.

- *Put everything on the table.* Fight the tendency to hide our struggles. If the electric company is about to shut off the power, let your Allies know. If your child is being expelled from school, let your Allies know. Allies are not there to criticize or to solve problems, but they are there to be intentional friends. Circles is a safe place to get real ... real fast.

- *Table big decisions.* When people live in survival mode, they can become accustomed to making short-term decisions to try to alleviate painful and difficult circumstances. Staying put and putting everything on the table can feel counterintuitive. Big, sweeping decisions—move, quit, run, etc.—can feel more familiar and "wiser" than doing the opposite. However, Circles data collection and research demonstrates that Circle Leaders who remain in a Match Circle with their Allies for 18 months realize the greatest level of outcomes.

Rather than providing stop-gap supplies and information for a limited time (transactional), Circles taps into people's personal goals and dreams for a better life (relational) and then provides genuine support and motivation (friendships) as Circle Leaders turn their dreams into action plans (transformational). This takes place through weekly support meetings, progress reports, and accountability to others.

Thank You for Sharing

For many people raised without sufficient resources, hearing and acknowledging their own voice takes practice. Believing their own voice takes courage. Acting on their own voice takes a leap of faith. Fortunately, their friends and Allies at Circles are always there to support and encourage them to leap again.

Circles provides a place to go where Circle Leaders know they will be listened to, appreciated, and valued. Through the support of a caring community and committed Allies, Circle Leaders grow accustomed to being heard. They become familiar with receiving support and encouragement in ways they may not have experienced. This can-do community builds new confidence. We have seen so many Circle Leaders, who at first would hardly speak in public, begin to find their voice in Circles.

In their book, *Switch: How to Change Things When Change is Hard,* authors Dan Heath and Chip Heath share that one of the biggest obstacles we face is that our brains are wired for conflict more than we realize. We are innately problem focused.

Since there will always be problems to which we can turn our attention, remaining problem focused can be: "… a recipe for inaction, for paralysis." What is called for is a switch in focus from problems to what the authors call bright spots: "When you find a bright spot, your mission is to study it and clone it."

Circles understands that to move the needle on poverty rather than continuing to manage it, we must turn our focus on scaling solutions— find the bright spots of success, study them, and clone them. With a specific endgame established, we can quantify what works and do more of that—taking action steps rather than arguing over faction cells.

Impact

Circles has been researched by numerous individuals and institutions, including Stephen Aigner, Ph.D. from Iowa State University: Mary Jane Collier, Ph.D., and Brandi Lawless, Ph.D., University of New Mexico; University of Michigan MBA team led by Michael Gordon, Ph.D.; Wilder Research; Vital Smarts; and Gordon Hannah, Ph.D. These formative evaluations have provided invaluable insights that have led to ongoing improvements of the model and of better results.

Circles provides Circles chapters with an online data system to measure progress being made by Circle Leaders. The most recent results can be found on the Circles® USA website (circlesusa.org). The following shows the percentage of increase in earned income as people continue with Circles over time.

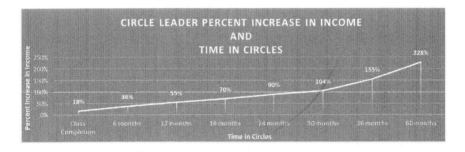

As illustrated, people make a slow and steady climb out of poverty. Because Circles is relationship based and seeks to address the underlying causes of poverty that are within the control of families, we also measure other factors, such as reliable transportation, safe and secure housing, number of people someone can count on, and educational attainment. Each of these factors goes up over time.

Resources

While policy changes are essential to reducing poverty rates, much can be done in the meantime to help people cope better with what they have. Allies can bring an exceptional level of new resources—ideas, inspiration, and connections to Circle Leaders. In the first Circles chapter, 160 cars were donated by Allies from the community. People were then able to find and keep jobs more easily as well as to go back to school to earn more income.

What is most important is that people show up for weekly meetings and keep moving forward on their goals. A recent study on retention showed that 77% of those who start Circles are still involved 18 months later. Again, this is a testament to the importance of a relationship-centric approach that brings new resources to the table in order to achieve better results.

Expanding Circles

Circles® USA has more than 50 nationally known community programs using Circles: United Way, The Salvation Army, Goodwill, Community Action Agencies, churches, and many more. As Circles expands, continued refinement of the Circles' model ensures it can be distributed through a variety of major program associations.

Circles has projects taking place in every region of the United States and in parts of Canada. It is holistic, long-term, comprehensive, and focused on solving the underlying problems of poverty. It taps into the enormous potential of community volunteers, coupled with the coordination of existing community programs.

Before Circles, I was struggling. I still struggle, from time to time, but what I have now that I didn't a year-and-a-half ago is support. Circles has helped me learn how to budget and save money—which was never in my vocabulary before—and my Allies have supported me along the way. I have been able to find resources in the community that I never knew existed. I didn't know or care how bad credit would affect my life. I didn't know how to do a resume. As a single mom of three, living paycheck to paycheck, you feel alone—especially living away from family.

I never thought about future goals. My mindset was to make it through the day. I grew up in poverty, and my parents grew up in poverty.

My dad mainly worked in the coal mines. My mom was a stay-at-home parent for most of my childhood. We moved a lot growing up. They were good parents, but they had alcohol issues.

I'm trying to break the cycle, so my children don't grow up in poverty. I want them to be successful in life.

Now, I have goals set for myself and for my family. This program has absolutely changed my outlook on life, and it has changed my children's future.

I am not alone in this world. I thank everyone in Circles. Without all of them, and the knowledge I have received in Circles, I would still be in the hole I was in less than two years ago.

Amber Schwingdorf, Circle Leader

Chapter 8

Begin the End of Poverty

Circles helped my mom budget and plan our money. We don't run out of milk money now. If we run out of milk, we can get it instead of waiting a week when we have money again.

Youth participant whose mom is a Circle Leader

A Call to Action and Adventure

If you are ready to take the next step to end poverty in your community one family at a time, we invite you to join us.

Next steps:

- **Contact Circles**
  Go to circlesusa.org or call (888) 232-9285 to find out how you can become involved.

- **Learn More**

  Scott C. Miller, founder and CEO of Circles® USA, has written several books on how to eliminate poverty. His books, *The Circles Story* and *Until It's Gone*, include more real-life stories from Circles chapters across North America. Go to circlesusa.org.

- **Start a Chapter**

  Circles® USA will help you develop a solid foundation for success through a customized planning process, training programs, data systems, marketing platforms, best-practices catalog, coaching, materials, and peer-to-peer support services. Go to circlesusa.org to start a chapter.

- **Continue the Conversation**

  Connect with others online to continue the conversation. Go to circlesusa.org to connect.

Glossary

Ally: A volunteer who assists a Circle Leader in achieving his or her goals. The commitment is to meet at least once a month for 18 months.

Appreciation: At the close of each Circles meeting, an appreciation is a positive comment each participant shares about another person in attendance: "I appreciate you, Mary, because …"

Back Doors: Because change can be hard, "slipping out a back door" is an expression for returning to our comfort zones rather than continuing to pursue our SMART goals.

Benefits: Persons inclined to focus on what society can do to improve the circumstances of groups of people.

Big View: One of a Circles' weekly meetings focused on addressing large-scale barriers, i.e., Cliff Effect, housing, transportation, etc.

Bonding Capital: Connections a person has with friends and family.

Bootstraps: Persons inclined to focus on what individuals can do to improve their own circumstances.

Bridging Capital: Connections a person has with individuals other than friends and family.

Circles Location: Venue that holds weekly meetings of up to 25 Circle Leaders.

Circle Leader: Families or individuals who are working to journey out of poverty with support from Allies, have completed Circle Leader Training, and are ready to share their time and stories to help others and change the community.

Cliff Effect: The financial precipice that those closest to escaping poverty face when a modest increase in earned income leads to the elimination of benefits at a steeper rate than the increase in income.

Matched Circle: A Circle Leader and two or more Allies who meet to work on the Circle Leader's dreams, plans, and goals.

New and Good: Shared at the opening of a Circles meeting, each participant shares something positive with the group—something that is both "new" and "good."

Poverty IQ: Understanding poverty (living with insufficient resources) either through personal experience or through relationships with individuals who have experienced it firsthand.

Prosperity IQ: Understanding prosperity (acquiring, managing, and increasing resources) either through personal experience or through relationships with individuals who have experienced it firsthand.

Reciprocity: Two-way relationships where everyone gives and receives.

SMART Goals: Specific, measurable, achievable, relevant, and time-bound.

> **Open-ended Goal**: Lose weight.

> **SMART Goal**: Lose 10 pounds (specific, measurable,

achievable) in 12 weeks (time-bound) by implementing and maintaining the following healthy diet and exercise regimen (relevant). Here are my "back doors" and my plan for closing them.

Social Capital: Connections with resources, peers, and individuals outside of one's peer group. These include linking to community resources; bonding with friends and family; and bridging with individuals other than their friends and family. All three are needed for families and individuals to move out of poverty.

The Federal Poverty Guidelines (FPG): Issued annually by the Department of Health and Human Services and used to determine financial eligibility for federal programs. FPG varies by family size but not by elderly status. It is the same for the 48 contiguous states and Washington, D.C., but is different for Alaska and Hawaii. FPG is issued at the end of January for that year.

The Federal Poverty Level (FPL): Issued annually by the Census Bureau and used primarily for statistical purposes. FPL varies by family size and elderly status. It is the same for all 50 states. FPL is issued based on the poverty measurements from the previous year.

Made in the USA
Middletown, DE
09 August 2018